D0075857

THE BEGINNINGS OF RELIGION

THE BEGINNINGS OF RELIGION

An Introductory and Scientific Study

by

E. O. JAMES,

M.A., D.LITT., PH.D., HON. D.D., F.S.A.

PROFESSOR OF THE HISTORY AND PHILOSOPHY OF RELIGION IN THE UNIVERSITY OF LONDON, AND FELLOW OF UNIVERSITY COLLEGE. SOMETIME WILDE LECTURER IN NATURAL AND COMPARATIVE RELIGION IN THE UNIVERSITY OF OXFORD. EDITOR OF "FOLK-LORE."

GREENWOOD PRESS, PUBLISHERS
WESTPORT, CONNECTICUT

Library of Congress Cataloging in Publication Data

James, Edwin Oliver, 1886-
The beginnings of religion.

Reprint of the 1950 ed., which was issued as no. 8 of Hutchinson's university library: World religions.
Includes bibliographies.
1. Religion, Primitive. I. Title.
BL430.J29 1973 291'.042 72-11737
ISBN 0-8371-6706-X

THIS VOLUME IS NUMBER 8 IN
HUTCHINSON'S UNIVERSITY LIBRARY

Originally published in 1950 by Hutchinson's University Library, London, New York

Reprinted with the permission of Hutchinson & Co., Publishers, Ltd.

Reprinted in 1973 by Greenwood Press, Inc.,
51 Riverside Avenue, Westport, CT 06880

Library of Congress catalog card number 72-11737
ISBN 0-8371-6706-X

Printed in the United States of America

10 9 8 7 6 5 4 3 2

CONTENTS

PREFACE

As this is an early volume in the section devoted to the study of religion in a series of educational books, under the general title of The Universities Library, a twofold aim has been kept in mind. In the first place an attempt has been made to provide an intelligible introduction to a somewhat complex and still not very precise or widely understood aspect of scientific inquiry. And secondly, to construct a background of primitive ritual and belief against which the more developed religions of mankind in their various aspects and attributes can be placed by subsequent writers in the series.

The investigation of the origin and development of religion, of course, is not confined to a single method of approach, but, nevertheless, it would seem to be appropriate to begin with a survey of the raw material which a skilled band of craftsmen will fashion in their own ways according to their several interests, purposes and expert knowledge. Clearly this is a task not for one person but for a team, and all that has been undertaken in the present volume is a survey of the beginnings of a long and complicated process which has played a determining part in each and every phase of human thought and culture throughout the ages.

It is true that science and history are inadequate alone to establish the validity of religious phenomena, and in the quest of truth the findings of philosophy and theology are all-important, as will be shown in other volumes. But since it is the business of the Science of Man to endeavour to discover the early phases and fundamental nature of religion as a human institution, the comparative study of the discipline carried out in the anthropological spirit and by aid of its methods, throws a good deal of light on the essential function of religion in the cohesion and stabilization of society at critical junctures in the life of a community. And this is a matter that is much in the minds of thinking men and women to-day who are asking the crucial question, What is the place of religion in our modern culture? It will remain for others, as the series proceeds, to supply many of the answers, but at least it may have been worth while initiating the inquiry in relation to the so-called primitive or simple cultures brought under review in this volume; especially as it is in these societies that the social function of religion is very apparent.

Not being in the nature of a text-book or technical treatise, it has not been thought necessary or desirable to introduce an elaborate scheme of documentation in the text. In the bibliographies at the end of each chapter the serious student who is anxious to pursue a more detailed study of the subject will find the material he needs. For his further guidance references have been given in the text where it has seemed that particular sources of information should be indicated. These can be ignored by the general reader without any inconvenience since, to avoid any interruption in the narrative, they have been added in the form of footnotes. Different points of view have been stated, I hope without prejudice and quite fairly, as it is most important in a book intended primarily for students beginning the study of the subject, and in a field of investigation where so much is tentative and experimental, that interpretation should not be made to appear as evidence, or the author's pet theories foisted upon unsuspecting readers as final and established conclusions. I have not hesitated, however, to state the point of view which the independent study of the problems under consideration for more than thirty years has led me to adopt, and to draw my own inferences from the available data.

E. O. JAMES.

King's College,
Strand, W.C.2.

INTRODUCTION

SINCE the middle of the last century when evolution became an approved principle in biology the attempt to discover the beginnings of human institutions and to trace in outline their development from very simple forms, has made an irresistible appeal to inquiring minds. The discoveries of prehistoric archæology bringing to light the imperishable remains of Early Man have stimulated the study of his cultural achievements by analogies drawn from existing groups of people in various parts of the world who are, or until recently were, living under conditions similar to those which are believed to have prevailed when the human race first emerged from its mammalian ancestry. But however fascinating may be the quest of beginnings and bygones, when the available evidence is as scanty and precarious as that on which the reconstruction of human origins inevitably rests, a good deal must be in the nature of conjecture, or at best disciplined scientific inference, so that it is hardly surprising if the first attempts have required a considerable amount of revision in the light of fuller knowledge.

Evolution and the Idea of Progressive Development

Under the inspiration of Darwin's brilliant exposition in 1859 of the 'origin of species' through a process of natural selection, and the "descent of man" from inferior forms of life, the dictum of Herbert Spencer, "from the simple to the complex, and from the homogeneous to the heterogeneous," seemed to be an established principle applicable to each and every domain of existence. In the human sphere the theory was supported by the discovery of a progressive sequence of types ranging from anthropoids through the ape man, or *Pithecanthropus erectus* of Java, to the cave species (*Homo Neanderthalensis*) as the precursor of the modern type of man (*Homo sapiens*) at the peak of the series. A similar evolution was suggested by the continuous succession of prehistoric flint and stone cultures extending from the debatable roughly chipped eoliths from the plateau-gravels on the North Downs and the more convincing early examples of alleged human artefacts known as 'rostro-carinates' found beneath the Red Crag at Foxhall near Ipswich and at Cantal in France, to the unquestionable hand-axes and flake and blade industries brought to light in great numbers from river gravels, glacial deposits and inhabited caves in Western Europe. Here again it appeared that the Spencerian principle was maintained since the tools began as very simply chipped nodules, or cores, and gradually were fashioned with greater dexterity as mastery over the material was gained. Then complex techniques with secondary working and pressure flaking were evolved which reached their climax in the magnificent laurel-leaf blades found at Solutré in France and thence across the Central plain to the Eurasian steppes.

As investigation proceeded, however, while the idea of progressive development in material culture and creative achievement has never been abandoned or denied as a generalization, the dictum of Herbert Spencer has had to be considerably modified to fit the facts, as these have become known. The discovery in 1912, for example, in the Sussex Weald at Piltdown of a very ancient human skull resembling in several important features the modern type of man (*Homo sapiens*), followed by similar finds in contemporary deposits as widely dispersed as Pekin, Kenya and Swanscombe in Kent, suggests a collateral development of different types rather than a unilineal ascent from the apes to cave man through the Java *Pithecanthropus*.

The archæological evidence, again, although it shows a growing complexity in technique, has now become infinitely more complicated than when the French sites suggested a continuous succession of cultures named after the type stations—Chellean, Acheulean, Mousterian, Aurignacian, Solutrian and Magdalenian. To-day a new pattern is in process of production with two groupings in the Old Stone Age and a third emerging later to join them, with core implements and those made from flakes less clearly differentiated than in the earlier scheme. Similarly, in the domain of tomb construction at the dawn of civilization (i.e., in the Neolithic and Bronze Age), the evolutionary theory which derived the multi-chambered passage-graves, corridor-tombs and vast corbelled vaults, and so-called "beehives" of the Aegean area, from small single chambers, known as dolmens, composed of upright slabs covered with a capstone, has been abandoned as a totally inadequate simplification of a highly complex problem. Indeed, it is now maintained by many archæologists that the classical typology began at the wrong end. So far from the simple dolmens of Portugal, Brittany and the western seaboard being the starting point of a 'megalithic culture,' they are now thought by many archæologists to represent degenerate derivations of the great graves of the Aegean and the Eastern Mediterranean. Be this as it may, the reversal shows the change that has taken place in recent years in the evolutionary ideas respecting the development of human culture even in the material sphere.

It is hardly surprising, therefore, that a corresponding reaction has occurred in the anthropological study of institutions, customs and beliefs. In the wake of the Darwinian revolution heroic efforts were made to maintain a scientific approach to the investigation of religion as an aspect of culture by assuming strata in the development of thought and practice as clearly defined as those exhibited by the geological record of the earth. Examples of savage cults and rites were collected from all parts of the world with a view to deducting evolutionary sequences and laws, and so of reconstructing the past by the data surviving in the present among peoples in a primitive state of culture.

Even before the publication of *The Origin of Species* in 1859, the French philosopher Auguste Comte (1798-1857) had introduced the comparative method in the study of social and religious institutions in an attempt to establish what he called 'the Law of the Three Stages'. According to this scheme, man began by explaining the phenomena of nature *theologically* in terms of fetichism, polytheism and monotheism, the vague notion of a separate will animating material objects (fetichism) becoming generalized in a belief in many gods acting through things without the things being themselves alive (polytheism, as he used the term), until finally everything is brought under a single abstract will (monotheism). At this point the theological interpretation of the universe is said to pass into the higher stage of *metaphysics*, the personal will giving place to abstract essences and powers as repetitions of the gods of the previous epoch. As this furnishes no real explanation of phenomena, it constitutes a temporary phase leading to the final goal in the *positive* or scientific thought, occupying itself solely with the facts of experience and the laws which they reveal. As each group of sciences enters into the next higher group, so the whole science of material nature gets its reason and end in the highest concept, namely, the service of humanity, whose life can be modified because its laws are known. Moreover, taking social organization as a whole, a nexus is said to exist between each leading group of phenomena and other leading groups so that the early stages of civilized groups may be observed among primitive peoples. Each group, in fact, on this hypothesis, is bound to pass through these three stages by the same steps at varying rates, but uniformly independent of diversities of race or environment because the human mind is invariable in its operations.

The widespread influence exercised by this new 'positive philosophy' in the first half of the nineteenth century could hardly fail to have important repercussions on the anthropological approach to the development of human institutions and beliefs when the revolution brought to a head by Darwin in 1859 had shown that culture and religion could be studied scientifically as part of the evolutionary progress. As Marett has said, "anthropology is the child of Darwin," and, therefore, it was committed in the days of its youth to an evolutionary outlook in the study of the human race and its institutions. Consequently, starting from the assumption that man has arisen from savagery to civilization in very much the same way as other organisms have advanced in an orderly sequence from lower to higher forms of life and organization, a system of classification had to be devised to explain the similarities and distinctions manifest in rites, beliefs, customs, institutions, implements and other aspects of culture.

The Comparative Method

The first systematic attempt to explain causal connexions between cultural traits was made by Edward Burnett Tylor (1832-1917) who in 1865 published his pioneer work, *Researches into the Early History of Mankind.* In this volume as an orthodox Darwinian he distinguished the 'lower' from the 'higher' in the development of culture in a purely stratigraphical sense, and attributed similarities in beliefs and customs to "the like working of men's minds under like conditions," though "sometimes it is a proof of blood relationship or intercourse, direct or indirect between the races among whom it is found." He allowed for the possibility of decline but the history of mankind he thought "has been on the whole a history of progress," the forward view and onward gait having always prevailed. Civilization being regarded as always progressive by its very nature, it was only a question of whether the upward trend was mainly the result either of independent invention or of borrowing from outside. Both processes were at work, and in two areas comparatively near each other the progress, it was alleged, will be stimulated by interaction, whereas in widely separated regions, such as Asia and Africa, intervention must come from within as spontaneous metamorphoses proceeding according to definite laws and producing a fixed sequence of successive stages as distinctly stratified as the earth on which man lives.

Thus, in his great treatise on *Primitive Culture* published in 1871, Tylor concentrated his attention on the laws of human nature along the lines laid down by Comte, taking as his basic assumptions that (1) the history of culture began with the appearance on earth of a semi-civilized race of men, and from this state of culture has proceeded in two ways, backward to produce savages, and forward to produce civilized men ; (2) everywhere and at all times the human mind operates according to specific laws of thought and action rather than as a result of cultural connexions. But (3) notwithstanding the universal progressive movement in history, a time-lag occurs in cultural change so that there is a *survival* of the backward as well as of the fittest with the result that earlier and more primitive traits and ideas are to be found not only among savages on the fringes of civilization but in the form of folk-lore, defined by Andrew Lang as "the study of survivals," within the borders of advanced communities.

Animism as a "Minimum Definition of Religion"

In his *Researches into the Early History of Mankind* the problem of religious origins was not discussed, but in the following year (1866) Tylor contributed an article to the *Fortnightly Review* on "the Religion of Savages" in which he first called attention to the idea of animism, or the theory of souls, as a fundamental concept in primitive belief. During the five years that separated this article from the publication of *Primitive Culture* his thought had been developing on the problem of religion and taken shape in the form of a definite and far-reaching hypothesis which he set forth in detail in his great book. He had come to the conclusion that "the belief in spiritual beings" constitutes the "minimum definition of religion" and essential source of all the various systems of spirits and gods in low races. "It cannot be positively asserted," he says, "that every existing tribe recognizes the belief in spiritual beings" or indeed possesses "the defined minimum of religion". But from the immense mass of accessible evidence we have to admit, he thought, that "the belief in spiritual beings appears among all low races with whom we have attained to thoroughly intimate acquaintance ; whereas the assertion of absence of such belief must apply either to ancient tribes, or to more or less imperfectly described modern ones." [1]

At a low level of culture, thinking men, in his opinion, are deeply impressed by the difference between a living body and a dead one, and curious concerning the causes of waking and sleep, trance, disease and death. In nature there appears to be an all-pervading life and will while even inanimate objects seem to be animated by personal souls. Moreover, there are those human shapes which appear in dreams and visions. Looking at these two groups of phenomena, the ancient philosophers, he suggested, "probably made their first step by the obvious inference that every man has

[1] Page 425.

two things belonging to him, namely a life and a phantom". Both are in close connexion with the body but separable from it ; the one (i.e., the life) enabling it to think and act, the other (the phantom) existing as the second self, "a thin substantial human image" flashing from place to place as the ghost-soul during life and after death appearing in the likeness of its corporeal owner and entering the bodies of other men, of animals and even of inanimate objects. Similarly, personality and life are ascribed to the sun and stars, trees, rivers, winds and clouds. Therefore, they too are treated as living intelligent beings, "talked to—propitiated, punished for the harm they do". [1]

Between these two conceptions of a pervading life and an animating principle in the form of a personal soul there is a distinction which Tylor failed to perceive. Dreams and visions cannot be made to account for the entire phenomena, as he imagined, since they do not explain the idea of the soul as a reflection, a shadow and the expiring breath, or its association with a vital organ of the body such as the heart or the head, or with the blood as the life principle. In short, the doctrine of animism represents a complex attempt to interpret the material and spiritual aspect of the phenomenal world by resolving the universe into a fundamental dualism of body and soul. But this dichotomy is the product of a long process of conceptual thinking and philosophical reflection which took its rise in Greece in the sixth century B.C. rather than in primitive society. In dividing Reality into the invisible permanent world of ideas grasped by the reason and the transient phenomenal order visible to us and known through the sense, Plato developed doctrines which Heraclitus, Anaxagoras, the Orphics and the Pythagoreans had borrowed from an earlier stratum of thought, very much as in their turn Descartes, Leibnitz, Lotze and McDougall went back through the Scholastics in the Middle Ages to the animistic ideas of Plato and Aristotle. But while it cannot be denied that the notion of, soul or ghost, or spirit is a genuinely primitive belief, as we shall see, the interpretation placed upon it by Tylor belongs essentially to the

[1] *Op cit.*, page 477.

philosophy of religion. This, indeed, he recognized, describing animism as "the groundwork of the philosophy of religion from that of savages up to that of civilized men," but, nevertheless, it was for him the centre and source of all religious belief and practice.

While animistic ideas may have been latent from the beginning they do not seem to have been expressed in the manner suggested by this hypothesis. Furthermore, the primitive mind if not as 'mystical' and 'pre-logical' as the French anthropologist, Lévy Bruhl and his followers, endeavoured to prove, is certainly not prone to clear-cut evolutionary sequences of thought such as predominated among scientifically trained thinkers in the latter part of the last century. To them it seemed that starting with animism as 'the minimum definition' the rest could be explained quite satisfactorily either, as Herbert Spencer suggested, by reviving the theory of the Greek romantic writer Euhemerus, who in the third century B.C. maintained that the Olympian gods arose through the veneration of heroes, warriors, benefactors and kings raised to divine rank after death ; or, as J. G. Frazer contended, by the development of monotheism from polytheism and animism as a result of the alleged instinctive craving after simplification and unification of ideas.

It soon became apparent, however, that, like the unilateral ascent of man from the apes, these evolutionary interpretations of religious development could not be maintained in the light of the accumulating evidence. In 1898 Andrew Lang in an important book entitled *The Making of Religion* called attention to the existence of "High Gods among Low Races" who were neither spirits nor ghosts, but rather, in Matthew Arnold's phrase, "magnified non-natural men". "Our conception of God," he said, "descends not from ghosts but from the Supreme Being of non-ancestor worshipping peoples". This he realized did not fit into the evolutionary sequence suggested by Tylor and his contemporaries as an all-embracing account of primitive religion. Anthropomorphic deities from the Australian All-Fathers to the Greek Olympian gods are no more animistic in origin and nature than the Holy One of Israel or the Sovereign Ruler of Islam, while, as

Marett maintained, the notion of spiritual beings is really too clearly defined a concept to be a satisfactory "minimum definition of religion". "Savage religion," he pointed out, "is something not so much thought out as danced out, that, in other words, it develops under conditions, psychological and sociological, which favour emotional or motor processes, whereas ideation remains relatively in abeyance".[1]

Animatism

To differentiate the tendency of the primitive mind to treat the inanimate, in so far as it is held to be sacred, as if it were pervaded with life and will, from the animistic belief in personal souls animating natural objects, Marett in 1899 coined the term "Animatism". Not being a scientifically trained thinker, the savage, he thought, is quite incapable of the refinements of thought involved in Tylor's theory. He is conscious of the phenomena of life, growth and movement as manifested in the animation of nature. Therefore, it is argued, the notion of being alive is logically distinct from and historically and psychologically more rudimentary than that of animation interpreted in terms of spirits and souls, and when life is manifested in unfamiliar and mysterious circumstances it is given an animatistic rather than an animistic significance. In other words, it is regarded as what we should describe as a supernatural occurrence.

As early as 1892 J. H. King had called attention to the sense of wonder in the presence of the mysterious as a primary emotion in religious experience giving rise to a consciousness of frustration. To overcome the dangers of uncontrollable natural forces the aid of protecting agencies was sought by primitive folk which at first, as he maintained, were "the mere expositions of luck according as the objects or acts were associated with corresponding results". In this way he thought a series of false sentiments arose in the human mind which found expression in (a) a theory of spirits and (b) the idea of luck, 'fear of uncanny evil or the desire for canny good,' which he regarded as the source of all religion, prior to ideation. King's significant book, *The Supernatural: its*

[1] *The Threshold of Religion* (London, 1914), page 31.

Origin, *Nature and Evolution*, passed, however, unnoticed until it was rescued from oblivion by Fr. Schmidt in 1912, but it shows the direction in which thought was moving at the end of the last century when Marett in his brilliant exposition of "preanimistic religion" in his paper before the Folk-lore Society in 1899, arrested attention on this aspect of the problem.

It soon became apparent that Tylor's theory of spiritual beings was too specialized and intellectualized a concept to represent the origin of religion. Something at once wider and vaguer was needed along the lines of the doctrine of animatism, while room must also be found for Lang's "High Gods of low races". Lang was inclined to associate wonder-working power (*mana*) more with magic than religion and to regard it as relatively late as a generalization, but, as will be seen in the next chapter, this is not borne out by the evidence. In arriving at this conclusion he seems to have been following Frazer (with whose animistic theories he had little sympathy), who maintained that magic and religion were different in kind as well as in origin.

Starting from Hegel's wholly *a priori* contention that an 'age' of pure magic preceded an 'age' of religion, Frazer surmised that when the acuter minds detected the fatal flaw in the attempt of the magician to bend nature to his will by the sheer force of spells and enchantments, recourse was made to the propitiation or conciliation of powers superior to man believed to direct and control directly natural processes and human affairs. Thus, the priest became the lineal descendant of the medicine-man as the persuasive methods of sacrifice and prayer replaced the dictatorial incantations of the magic art.[1] But no evidence exists in support of the alleged transition from one principle of supercausation to the other. On the contrary, so far from religion having arisen out of the failure of the magician to exercise his powers successfully, the two disciplines in every known community occur side by side so that, as Frazer admits, the functions of priest and sorcerer often have not been differentiated. Prayers and spells, in fact, have been uttered almost in the

[1] *Golden Bough* (Part I, Magic Art), page 234.

same breath with an inconsistency characteristic of the emotional reactions of the primitive mind to the inexplicable and uncontrollable.

To represent the savage as an intellectualistic reasoner or framer of carefully thought out systems and schemes operating in logical and evolutionary sequence, is to misinterpret primitive mentality as thoroughly as to reduce him to a state of pre-logical mysticism. He is neither "perpetually spook-haunted", as Marett says, nor does he distinguish abstractly from "an order of uniform happenings and a high order of miraculous happenings. He is merely concerned to mark and exploit the difference when presented in the concrete".[1] Nature and the supernatural, magic and religion, animatism and animism, supreme beings and tribal ancestors, are all inextricably mixed up in a conglomerate rather than in clearly marked strata in the deposit we call primitive society. Psychologically animatism seems to be more rudimentary than animistic beliefs about spiritual beings and ghosts, and possibly historically it represents an earlier phase in religious development, but to work out chronologically a sequence of belief and custom as the geologist determines the history of the rocks is to attempt the impossible. Priority in type is not to be confused with priority in time, and while Marett's term 'pre-animistic' admittedly has a chronological reference, he was careful to point out that it does not necessarily presuppose "a pre-animistic era in the history of religion when animism was not and nevertheless religion of a kind existed."

The Development of Human Institutions

The workings of the human mind cannot be explained in terms of laws and processes applicable to the phenomena investigated by biologists, geologists and physicists because man's fundamental nature and attributes introduce important modifications in his reactions to his environment and the circumstances that make up his life not present in the growth of plants and animals, or in the evolution of the solar system and the changes in the crust of the earth. The customs,

[1] *Threshold of Religion*, page 109.

beliefs, institutions and material basis of life, which collectively make up human culture, have not developed as a series of spontaneous metamorphoses according to fixed laws in a regular sequence of successive stages because the conditions of their emergencies are psychological and sociological—that is to say, they emerge out of the mind and out of society—and have been subject to constant change by borrowing and transmission from one human group to another. Animism cannot be derived spontaneously from animatism and monotheism from polytheism any more than indiscriminate promiscuity can be made to pass into polygamy and thence to monogamy, because religious beliefs and human relationships are not subject to metamorphoses of this kind.

The Historical Method

Or, again, the attempt of a German school of anthropologists to establish a series of 'culture-horizons' (*kulturkreise*) within which religious and social phenomena are said to have developed, apart from the lack of confirmatory archæological evidence, is beset by the difficulty of arraying the 'culture-strata' chronologically on a really satisfactory basis of classification. Thus, it is alleged that the Pygmies represent an important element in the earliest substratum, or *Urkultur*, as a distinct race of 'dawn men' preserving all the principal traits of *primeval* man. But, in fact, they appear to be merely a dwarf variety of existing stocks resembling in all essential points the tall races, having been reduced in stature by the poverty of their food supply and other topographical conditions tending towards arrested development. Moreover, it is by no means clear that the so-called 'culture spheres' are really composed of closely inter-related traits woven together into a definite 'pattern' like the ritual that is centred in the Annual Festival (to which we shall return later), or the beliefs and practices that collectively make up an organized religion such as Christianity, Islam or Buddhism, or a modern political régime (e.g., Communism or Fascism), which have spread over wide areas from original centres through a process of diffusion and adaptation.

That customs, ideas and traits have spread and developed

in this way while others have degenerated and finally disappeared, is of course a fact, and a very important fact, in human history. Thus, to take an example from primitive society, quoted by Tylor, the mechanical device known as the piston-bellows unquestionably was a Malayan invention carried by the Malays in the course of their migrations to various places in the Malay Archipelago and the adjacent Asiatic mainland. But useful arts and articles of this nature, as Rivers has shown in case of the canoe, bow and arrow and pottery-making, have disappeared in some of the islands of the Pacific. By an analytical study of material traits, religious beliefs and institutions, and social organization it is possible to work out historical reconstructions of the movements of peoples and vicissitudes of cultural development in intimately related areas. Care has to be taken, however, in the use of this 'historical method' that a genuine diffusion has occurred, particularly in the case of alleged 'culture patterns', lest independently invented devices and ideas arising out of local causes and geographical conditions be confused with the spread of customs and beliefs.

The aim of historical investigation is to give a systematic description of the sequence of events which have some permanent value and significance in relation to the totality of happenings. To be remembered, recorded and passed on from one place or generation to another, objects, events and beliefs must have an interest, meaning and use for the community as a whole, or for a particular section of it. Thus, in primitive society, since the things that matter are given permanence in ritual, myth, and the traditional lore of the tribe, the study of the established rites and mythology, sanctions and organization, afford a clue to the past as well as providing a record of what is going on in the present. But before these descriptive snapshots can be transformed into a cinematograph film reconstructing the past in chronological sequence, each element has to be analysed in relation to its cultural history. No classification or comparison of rites, customs and beliefs can be satisfactory which does not take into account the internal lines of development, the movement of peoples and external modifying influences, any more than an examination of existing rocks is sufficient to determine the manner in which the strata were laid down in former times.

The Primitive and the Prehistoric

To assume that it is impossible to know anything at all about the religion and other institutions of mankind prior to the rise of civilization in the Ancient East in the fourth millennium B.C., or to assert that up to that point 'natural man' was virtually devoid of all culture except for a few flint implements, is to dismiss or ignore all the data now available from archæological sources, and to leave completely in the air the anthropological material among existing races in a primitive state of culture. The word 'primitive', it is true, should not be confused with 'primeval', but some term is required to describe modern peoples who have survived throughout the ages under conditions of life and environment not very different from those that obtained in Palæolithic and Neolithic times, prior to the rise of urban civilization and economy in the region sometimes known as the Fertile Crescent extending from Egypt through Palestine and Syria and the northern fringe of the Arabian desert to Mesopotamia and the Persian Gulf.

Notwithstanding the difficulties encountered when attempts are made to arrange this material in stratified layers with each stratum composed of the same elements of culture, the fact remains that in North America, Africa, Indonesia, Australia and the Pacific islands considerable human groups have survived little changed throughout the ages. Thus, the Tasmanians, the Australian aborigines, the pre-Dravidians jungle tribes of Southern India, the Veddas of Ceylon and the Bushmen of South Africa, the Eskimo and other peoples in the Arctic and sub-arctic tundra of Asia and America, and the Tierra del Fuegians of the extreme south of America, when they were first encountered by Europeans were 'Palæolithic' in the sense that they eked out a precarious existence gathering fruits and berries, hunting and fishing. They were devoid of any knowledge of the cultivation of crops or of using animals for domestic purposes, with the single exception of the dog which had become the companion of man in Australia.

Pygmies and Bushmen

For example, the African Pygmies live in small communities in the Congo forests without making any attempt to cultivate the soil, subsisting on the flesh of beasts, reptiles and birds which they hunt with bows and poisoned arrows. This restricted diet, as we have seen, probably has been very largely responsible for their dwarfed stature and arrested development, but while there is no reason to suppose that they represent the oldest surviving members of the human race from which all other stocks are descended, Dr. Haddon is probably right in regarding them as "the relics of a primitive form of Negro which at one time inhabited tropical Africa from the southern borders of the Sahara to the Zambesi-Congo watershed and from the east coast to the Atlantic".[1] South of the Zambesi the Bushmen, the cousins of the Pygmies of the Ituri forest, constitute the aboriginal element in the population, and the survivors of a very ancient race which formerly occupied practically the whole of the southern half of the continent.

From the Sahara which in Palæolithic times was an extensive grassland, waves of peoples migrated in a southerly direction and have left behind a succession of stone cultures located at such type stations as Stillenboach, Faureswith, and Wilton near Grahamstown, together with a series of cave paintings in Southern Rhodesia having affinities with the prehistoric art of Eastern Spain, and continuing as an integral part of the culture of the Bushmen until comparatively modern times. Indeed, down to the seventeenth century, the history of South Africa was virtually prehistory and the Bushmen are the oldest surviving members of the inhabitants, little changed in their ways of life and beliefs throughout the long period of their isolation. Living in caves or portable semi-circular huts, and organized on a tribal basis with hereditary chiefs, they have remained in a pre-agricultural state of development, subsisting on the chase,

[1] *The Races of Man* (Cambridge, 1929), page 43f.

edible roots and vegetables. They have some knowledge of pottery but they still carry water in ostrich eggs in which also they bury their stores as a precaution against bad seasons and dearth.

Australians, Tasmanians and Andamenese

The native tribes of Australia, again, have been completely cut off from all contacts with modern civilization until two hundred years ago. Thus, when Spencer and Gillen began their systematic investigation of their culture in 1894 they found them living under Stone Age conditions, devoid of metals, ignorant of any of the processes of growing crops, taming animals apart from the dog, and without clothes or permanent houses. In physical type they have affinities with the pre-Dravidians of Southern India, the Sakai of the Malay Peninsula, the Veddas of Ceylon and the Australoid groups in Java, New Guinea and possibly Borneo. It would seem probable, therefore, that they reached Australia by way of South-east Asia while they were still in a pre-Neolithic state of culture. The Tasmanians may represent an earlier and even less advanced migration of Negroids, akin to the Melanesians and Papuans, who were cut off by the formation of the Bass Strait. The Andamanese, the descendants of an original Negrito stock, likewise have been entirely isolated in their island home, and so determined to remain in seclusion that they are known to have attacked all strangers who landed or were wrecked on their unhospitable shores. So they too have maintained their culture intact and adapted it to the needs of their own environment without modification from outside influences.

The Eskimo

In the extreme limits of the hemisphere stretching across the North of America as far as Greenland, another homogeneous group of peoples have survived apparently little changed since they retreated with the ice and the reindeer to the arctic regions at the end of the Pleistocene period (*c.* 10,000 B.C.). Thus, on the Barren Grounds west of Hudson Bay the Caribou Eskimos still live under very primitive conditions hunting caribou and fishing in rivers and lakes, untouched by the various developments that have been taking place among the coastal peoples. If they are not actually the descendants of the Palæolithic Magdalenians, as has been suggested, they seem to represent a Proto-Eskimo stock characterized by snow houses, the absence of wooden utensils, and having a simple social life based on the family. At one time the Caribou culture covered the whole circumpolar area from Maine to Alaska in the sub-arctic tundra, and formed the basis of this prehistoric culture.

The North American Indians

To the east of the Hudson Bay the Algonquins and the Ojibwa, north of the Lakes, exhibit similar traits to those of the Western section occupied by the Déné tribes, but the neighbouring Iroquois reveal southern contacts and origin inasmuch as they supplement the hunting of deer, buffalo and bear, and sturgeon fishing, with the cultivation of maize and a complex social organization and vegetation cultus. Pottery is in use, and in the Eastern group agriculture becomes extensive, except in the extreme north. East of the Mississippi, in the south-west in the Pueblo area of Arizona and New Mexico and in Mexico proper, maize is the physical basis of the relatively advanced Neolithic type of civilization that prevails in this region. On the great barren plain between the Rocky Mountains and the Mississippi, on the other hand, a pre-agricultural culture survived dependent upon the buffalo and the bison with the horse replacing the dog for transport. In California the primitive culture which formerly was diffused throughout the region has been most in evidence among the hunting and fishing tribes of the centre, with their developed basketry, but with an absence of pottery-making, weaving and clan organization.

Thus, the apex of the indigenous civilization of America is the maize-producing central districts (Mexico, Guatemala, Yucatan, Columbia, Peru and Bolivia), and there an advanced urban culture flourished when the Spaniards arrived in the sixteenth century, the origins of which have given rise to much speculation. The Southern continent apparently received its culture from north of the Isthmus of Panama, and possibly from trans-Pacific influences, but the Incas, like the Aztecs, represent the final stage of a long development of agricultural civilization comparable to that which arose in the Near East when the farming communities, already established before the fifth millennium B.C., gave rise in due course (i.e., about 3400 B.C.) to the great civilizations in Egypt and Mesopotamia, and subsequently in the Indus valley in North-west India at Mohenjo-daro and Harappa, and other sites awaiting excavation.

The Diffusion of Culture

From these early centres the expansion of higher culture took place very gradually as traders, warriors, colonists and emissaries of various kinds went in search of new sources of wealth and territories to be conquered, while peasants pushed their fields further and further ahead in their need for fresh soil, and pastoralists extended their grazing grounds. Thus, customs, beliefs and institutions as well as practical techniques and material objects were diffused and adapted to the needs and circumstances of a new environment. Lack of contact between the centres of high civilization and the remote peripheries of their influence, left large areas in Africa, North America and the Pacific in complete or relative isolation as pockets in which the old ways have continued undisturbed. Consequently, when they were first visited in modern times by explorers, traders, missionaries and casual voyagers, the inhabitants were still not only living under what were virtually prehistoric conditions as regards their means of subsistence (i.e., either as gatherers of their food by hunting, fishing and collecting wild crops, or by the adoption of very simple methods of cultivation and herding), but they had evolved an economic, social and religious organization for the purpose of adapting themselves to their particular environment and creating an orderly communal existence. Therefore, if the data from these sources are insufficient for the determination of the origin and development of human institutions and beliefs in a strictly chronological sequence, they supply valuable material for the study of the *functions* performed by myth, ritual, morality and law as an essential part of the social machinery enabling human beings to live together in an orderly manner.

The Functional Method

It has become the habit in recent years for some investigators who concentrate on the social functions and implications of culture to decry as wholly irrelevant, and even "unscientific," all attempts at historical reconstructions and interest in the elucidation of origins. The only scientific method, it is said, is the experimental method, and that means the study of the contribution made by institutions such as religion to the formation and maintenance of a social order and its relations to its physical surroundings. But while unquestionably this aspect of the problem is of vital and fundamental importance, it does not necessarily rule out completely all concern for the way in which the existing order has come to take the form and shape it now presents, and what may have been the historical circumstances, causes and processes at work to produce these results. If, as Malinowski believed, religion can be shown to be intrinsically though indirectly connected with man's biological needs, it has still to be explained how the discipline has arisen and assumed this important rôle in human economy and found expression in such a variety of diverse systems and institutions within society. The present and the past, function and history, cannot be wholly separated the one from the other since they are manifestly interdependent. Therefore, while it is proposed in this volume to pay particular attention to the part played by religion as an essential element in the building up and consolidating of the structure of rudimentary society, the main purpose of the inquiry is that of constructing a background of primitive thought and practice against which the more developed faiths of mankind can be placed by other writers in this series.

BIBLIOGRAPHY

Burkitt, M.C. *South Africa's Past in Stone and Paint.* Cambridge, 1928.

Comte, A. *Cours de philosophie positive.* Paris, 1877. 4th Ed.
Dernan, S. S. *Pygmies and Bushmen of the Kalahari.* London, 1925.
Frazer, J. G. *The Golden Bough.* Vol. I. The Magic Art. Pt. I. 3rd Ed. London, 1911.
Haddon, A. C. *The Races of Man.* Cambridge, 1929.
Jenness, D. *The Indians of Canada.* Ottawa, 1933.
King, J. H. *The Supernatural, its Origin, Nature and Evolution.* London, 1892.
Joyce, T. A. *Mexican Archaeology.* London, 1914.
Kroeber, A. L. *Anthropology.* New York, 1923.
Lang, A. *The Making of Religion.* London, 1898.
Lévy-Bruhl, L. *How Natives Think.* E.T. London, 1926.
Lowie, R. H. *The History of Ethnological Theory.* London, 1938. *Culture and Ethnology.* New York, 1929.
Marett, R. R. *Anthropology.* London, 1911. (H.U.L.) *The Threshold of Religion.* London, 1914. *Tylor.* London, 1936.
Malinowski, B. Article "Culture" in *Encyclopaedia of the Social Sciences.* Vol. IV. 1931. *Argonauts of the Western Pacific.* London, 1922.
Radcliffe-Brown, A. R. *The Andaman Islanders.* Cambridge, 1922. *Religion and Society* (Henry Myers Lecture), 1945.
Rivers, W. H. R. *History of Melanesian Society.* Cambridge, 1914. *Psychology and Ethnology.* London, 1926.
Schmidt, W. *Origin and Growth of Religion.* London, 1931.
Seligman, C. G. *Races of Africa.* London, 1930. (H.U.L.)
Spencer, B., and Gillen, F. J. *Native Tribes of Central Australia.* London, 1899.
Tylor, E. B. *Researches into the Early History of Mankind.* London, 1865. *Primitive Culture.* London, 1871.
Weyer, E. M. *The Eskimo.* New Haven. 1932.
Wissler Clark. *The American Indian.* New York, 1922.

CHAPTER I

THE SACRED

FROM the preceding survey of the scientific approach to the study of religious origins it has become clear that absolute beginnings fall outside the scope of the anthropological data. Nevertheless, the word "beginnings" is a relative term when applied to institutions and ideas conditioned by time and change. If, for example, surviving peoples still living in what is virtually a prehistoric state of culture can be considered to have retained many of the traits and notions characteristic of Early Man, their customs and beliefs may be regarded as relatively nearer to those that prevailed at the threshold of religion than those which have gathered a theological and philosophical content among more developed and sophisticated folk in advanced civilizations. Although from the point of view of time, tribes and races commonly called "primitive" are as "modern" as ourselves, in their way of life, environment and thought they are manifestly nearer to the original outlook of mankind which underlies all the developed forms of cult and faith with which other writers in this series will deal. Therefore, the primitive approach to a transcendent order of reality reasonably may be made the starting-point of a comprehensive study of religion in its manifold aspects, provided that the limitations already set in the matter of chronological sequence be borne in mind. Moreover, as has been pointed out, a primitive community affords illuminating evidence of the way in which religion functions in a closely-knit society, and the purpose it has served, and perhaps may still exercise, in the cohesion of the social fabric. Thus, it becomes possible to estimate the fundamental nature and worth of the discipline and the part it has played in the development of culture and of the moral sense of the world.

The Nature of Religion in Primitive Society

For our present purposes religion may be regarded as the effective desire to be in right relations with a sacred transcendental order controlling human destinies and natural events which finds expression in a prescribed system of ritual and belief. Since the phenomenon has merged as an integral element in culture under conditions which are both psychological and sociological in character, it must be studied in its proper setting in relation to the mental atmosphere in which it has been produced and to the social order in which it functions. Long before the human mind makes any attempt at explaining or theorizing about the things it perceives but only dimly understands, it is aware of situations perplexing, inexplicable and mysterious which cannot be ignored. So long as nature and human events follow their normal course no particular reactions occur, but, as Dr. F. G. Moore says, "in a thousand ways the primitive is made aware that besides his fellow-men, friends or enemies, besides the animals which he pursues or which pursue him, in short, besides the things he is familiar with or more or less understands, there are around him other things that are outside his understanding as they are beyond his foresight or control".[1] Thus, he is led to make a distinction between the commonplace, or *noa* as would be said in the Pacific, and the mysterious, or *taboo*, without drawing any hard and fast line between what we should distinguish as the "natural" and the "supernatural". Neither of these expressions, in fact, really has any meaning when every object or event which arrests attention, or is inexplicable in terms of the normal is attributed to the sacred order. Cause and effect and agent and act are not clearly differentiated in the absence of a conception of the universality and continuity of natural causation.

In primitive states of culture the world is permeated with forces, influences and actions which though imperceptible to sense are thought to be real and tremendously powerful in the control of human destinies and natural processes. The whole universe belongs to one great system of interrelated and

[1] G. F. Moore, *The Birth and Growth of Religion* (Edinburgh, 1923), page 9.

inherent life other than and beyond the sensuous, and this is the unconscious expression of the religious emotion itself. In arousing the realization of a super-sensuous sacred order, or "otherness" beyond itself, society unquestionably plays a very important part in fostering the growth and development of religion by the power it exercises over the primitive mind. Nevertheless, as Dr. C. C. J. Webb has said, "the notion of the Divine is no mere mirage of social facts ; it is an explicit theory of the universe. The human mind necessarily conceives itself with the All, though it always starts in doing so with its immediate social environment, and only gradually realizes that this is not the dominant fact in the universe".[1] Now what Dr. Webb calls "the All" (using a philosophical term) may be described as "the Sacred," provided that the word is employed in its earlier meaning to indicate a *non-ethical* transcendental power or potency (cf. Latin *sacer*) manifest in mysterious and awe-inspiring occurrences.

The Notion of Mana

Thus, for example, in Melanesia any object, person or event behaving in an unusual manner, either for good or evil, is thought to be endowed with the power of the sacred or transcendental order known as *mana*. "If a man has been successful in fighting," Dr. Codrington tells us, "it has not been his natural strength of arm, quickening of eye, or readiness of resource that has won success ; he has certainly got the *mana* of a spirit or of some deceased warrior to empower him, conveyed in an amulet of a stone round his neck, or a tuft of leaves in his belt, in a tooth hung upon a finger of his bow hand, or in that form of words with which he brings supernatural assistance to his side. If a man's pigs multiply, and his gardens are productive, it is not because he is industrious and looks after his property, but because of the stones full of *mana* for pigs and yams that he possesses. Of course a yam naturally grows when planted, that is well known, but it will not be very large unless *mana* comes into play ; a canoe will not be swift unless *mana* is brought to

[1] *Group Theories of Religion and the Individual* (London, 1916), page 151.

bear upon it, a net will not catch many fish, nor an arrow inflict a mortal wound".[1]

Similarly, in Madagascar, everything that lies beyond the understanding of the Malagasy is said to be *andriamanitra* or *hasina*, just as in Africa among the Akikuyu it is *ngai*, or *mulunga* among the Yaos, east of Lake Nyassa. In North America the Iroquois "interpreted the activities of nature as the ceaseless strife between one *orenda* and another," *orenda* being a mystic force associated with will and intelligence comparable to the *wakonda*, or "power that moves," of the Sioux. Sometimes, however, *wakonda*, like the *manitu* of the neighbouring Eastern Algonquins, is equated with the idea of a personal god, while the Dakota assign *wakan* to everything that exhibits power, life, mystery and divinity.

In Morocco the Sultan as the viceregent of God owes his position to the *baraka*, regarded as an indwelling supernatural principle or soul-substance, which he inherits or appropriates from his predecessors. *Baraka*, in fact, is at once the sacredness, or 'holiness,' attributed to chiefs and saints, and to natural objects and places that have acquired sanctity in some way or another. It is present in blood as the life-principle, and upon it depends the efficacy of the 'conditional curse,' or *'ar*, so that any one who proves to be unfaithful to his promise, or breaks an oath, is liable to divine vengeance like the man who infringes a taboo. It is also responsible for making the crops abundant, giving fertility to women and prosperity to the country. Consequently, when this 'blessed virtue' is weak drought and famine ensue and the fruit falls from the trees before it is ripe. As a sacred contagion it can be transmitted to any object or place, such as a well, spring, rock or cave connected with a saint, which thereby acquires life-giving or medicinal qualities. The last portion of the crop, called 'the bride of the field,' is thought to be strongly impregnated with *baraka*, and, therefore, it is left untouched in order that its sacredness may be transmitted to the new corn of the next season. For the same reason threshing-floors are left unswept.

Behind all these terms, *mana*, *orenda*, *baraka* and so on—

[1] *The Melanesians* (Oxford, 1891), pages 118f.

and they could be multiplied almost indefinitely—there is the same fundamental conception of a transcendent order of sacredness, either personal or impersonal, external to man but operative in abnormal occurrences, uncanny objects, exceptional people and anything or anybody that has come into direct contact with supernatural potency. Thus, in the traditional account of the awe-inspiring phenomena experienced by the Israelites at Sinai (or Horeb), after their escape from Egypt, their god Yahweh (Jehovah) is said to have revealed his power in what seems to have been a volcanic eruption and an earthquake (cf. Exod. xix, 18, Deut. iv, 11f., Ps. lxviii, 7, 8, Judges v, 4f., II Kings xix, 8-14), while so sacred, was the mountain that the people were commanded not to go near it on penalty of death, and any man or beast that infringed the taboo would be so full of contagious sacredness that no hand might touch him lest it be consumed. Therefore, "bounds were set unto the people" and the mount became a sacred enclosure. Moreover, when Moses came down from its summit after he had conversed with his god, he put a veil on his face as a protection against profane influences, so great was his sanctity reflecting the sacredness, or *mana*, of Yahweh (Exod. xix, 12f., 23, xxxiv, 33f.).

The Sacredness of Sanctuaries

This sense of reverential awe in the presence of transcendent holiness recurs again in the Old Testament in the cult-legend of Jacob at Bethel recorded in the Book of Genesis (xxviii, 10-22). On his way to his uncle Laban in flight from the wrath of his brother Esau whom he had cunningly outwitted, the fugitive spent the night at an ancient megalithic sanctuary where, according to the narrative of the Northern Kingdom (E), he had a vision of a heavenly ladder with spiritual beings ascending and descending upon it. In the alternative version of the story current in the Southern Kingdom of Judah (J), Yahweh himself appeared to him in person, and in an articulate communication renewed the promise made to Abraham concerning the covenant with Israel. The sanctity of the sanctuary having been thus revealed, the Patriarch exclaimed, "how dreadful is this place! This is none other but the house of God, and this is the gate of heaven".

For the Northern Israelites Bethel was the most sacred spot on earth, comparable to Jerusalem among their Southern neighbours, and this story was told to show that it was actually the entrance to the true heavenly temple, whither ascent was made by means of the ladder in the vision. It is possible that the legend arose originally around a local physical feature since the hillside at Bethel rises up steeply in terraces towards the sky, and in the Fertile Crescent ladders and temple-towers were regarded as the means of ascent to the dwelling-place of the gods. Be this as it may, to mark its supreme sanctity Jacob is said to have set up one of the stones as a sacred pillar, or *mazzebah*, and to have poured oil on the top of it as an offering to the indwelling *numen*, or divine inhabitant, making a conditional vow to establish the sanctuary in return for divine protection and blessing. The dream, the circumstances of his journey, and the awe-inspiring surroundings in which he found himself, interpreting the story psychologically, produced in him a religious state of mind, in which emotional condition the experience of the *awful* was given evaluation in terms of supernatural power associated with a particular place and object.

The Category of the Numinous

As the Semites in the age to which the Hebrew patriarchal narratives refer had attained to the animistic belief in spiritual beings as separate entities, Jacob is represented as having interpreted his experience accordingly: "this is none other than the house of *El*," the spirit associated with the sanctuary. But the religious response to the sense of wonder and awe in the presence of transcendental sacredness is independent of any particular conceptual explanation in relation to spirits and gods. For Moses (or his interpreters in the pages of the Old Testament) the same pyschological situation was made the medium of the revelation of a Midianite deity, Yau or Yahweh, which had the effect of consolidating a loosely confederated group of tribes into a nation. For the Melanesians away in the islands of the Pacific, on the other hand, it is a sort of mystic force or power that works to effect everything that is beyond the ordinary efforts of man and the common processes of nature. For the ancient Latin farmers in Italy it represented collective and undistinguished powers or spirits associated with particular places or functions, for which the characteristic Latin name was *numina*. This term has been adopted by Dr. Otto to describe sacredness, or non-moral holiness, as a category of value and a state of mind peculiar to religion. Indeed, he regards the *numinous* as a mental condition and valuation "perfectly *sui generis* and irreducible to any other," comparable to beauty, truth and goodness.

"Therefore, like every absolutely primary and elementary datum, while it admits of being discussed, it cannot be strictly defined." In other words, religion is just "a numinous state of mind, and all ostensible explanations of the origin of religion in terms of animism, magic or folk psychology are doomed from the outset to wander astray and miss the real goal of their inquiry, unless they recognize this fact of our nature—primary, unique, and underivable from anything else—to be the basic factor and the basic impulse underlying the entire process of religious evolution".[1] Like the functional school of anthropologists, Otto is impatient of all attempts to discover the nature and meaning of religion from a study of its historical origins, and to sever it from its pyschological antecedents. His hypothesis, in fact, is almost a return to the theory of a religious instinct, since the numinous for him is virtually an instinctive reaction finding expression in a "transcendent Something, a real operative entity of a numinous kind, which later, as the development proceeds, assumes concrete form as a 'nomen loci', a daemon, an 'El,' a Baal, or the like".[2] It lies behind *mana*, sacredness, taboo and worship, and is summed up in the idea of the holy as a unique factor in creating and informing the complex attitudes which constitute the religious life of man.

[1] *The Idea of the Holy* (Oxford, 1928), pages 7, 15.

[2] *Op. cit.*, page 130.

The nature of this 'Something' is only gradually learned, but from the beginning it is felt as a transcendent presence standing over against the individual self-consciousness—the feeling that there is 'another' out beyond human consciousness, even when it is also felt as 'the within man'. In its presence the sense of 'creatureliness' is produced, of "self-abasement in nothingness before an overpowering, absolute might of some kind". But this *mysterium tremendum* or over-powering mystery has also within it the element of 'fascination', and so draws men towards it in mystical experience and communion. "The daemonic divine object may appear to the mind an object of horror and dread, but at the same time it is no less than something that allures with a potent charm, and the creature who trembles before it, utterly cowed and cast down, has always at the same time the impulse to turn to it, nay, even to make it somehow his own." [1]

This analysis of the experience of the numinous is open to the objection, however, that it is not an 'unnamed Something' which creates the reaction to the mysterious but anything that is uncanny, abnormal, awe-inspiring and beyond human control. Such an object or event may be perfectly familiar, but its manner of behaviour is inexplicable, or in some way transcends the ordinary and commonplace. Therefore, it appears to the primitive mind to belong to an order of reality outside its limited range of experience and understanding, interpreted simply in terms of the sacred, the supernatural, the transcendent. A combination of fear and reverend regard produces the emotion of awe which is not quite the same as *mana*, being a psychological condition rather than a mystic force or influence. It is called forth primarily by something greater, higher and beyond man which makes him conscious of his inferiority or 'creatureliness'. The cause not being malevolent it is not feared, yet its very sanctity renders it taboo in the sense of being approached with due care and respect. In this attitude to the object of religious regard, we may seek the birth of humility. Man must walk humbly and circumspectly in the heavenly places for many are the pitfalls

[1] *Op cit.*, pages 15, 31ff.

and dangers that await the unwary, the immodest and the profane in these lofty realms. "Woe is me ! for I am undone ; because I am a man of unclean lips and I dwell in the midst of a people of unclean lips." Nevertheless, such is the attraction of that which inspires awe as distinct from fear that, despite the taboos, men are drawn towards the sacred by means of a ritual technique wherein religion finds institutional expression.

Now all this is adequately comprehended in the term 'numinous' provided it is not made into a 'unique category' *sui generis*. The awareness of mystery is not confined to the religious consciousness since not all baffling situations, or uncanny objects, produce this effect. There must be a realization of helplessness, an inability to control the 'otherness' by human means, a sense of frustration combined with an 'other than itself' responsive to man's needs ; a 'beyond which is within' and around and above. But the domain of the sacred is neither 'wholly other' nor 'non-rational'. If it were completely transcendent it would not be within the reach of man at all, like Aristotle's "Unmoved Mover," and consequently it would be useless to attempt to establish beneficial relations with it, which is the essential aim of the religious reaction.

It is doubtless true that Otto has isolated the numinous in order to determine its real nature, but, nevertheless, he implies that below the level of conceptual thinking lies an emotional non-rational element in religious experience wholly different in kind from any other mental state. But there cannot be *a priori* sensation *sui generis*, for sensation is of the very essence of the *a posteriori*. Following Jakob Fries (1773-1843), he sees in the *a priori* our only organ of experience, and in its limits our essential limitation. Thus, he regards the religious thought of Plato as non-rational because the objects of religion are grasped by the "ideograms of myth, by enthusiasm or inspiration, by 'eros' or love, 'mania,' or the divine frenzy," not by conceptual thinking.[1] But in any valid theory of knowledge, intuition cannot be opposed to intelligence, and the intuitions of religion, though in their

[1] *Op. cit.*, page 98.

original striving they may be incapable of description in intellectual terms, spring from intellect no less than those of art and poetry. If a supra-rational evaluation is given to that which cannot be grasped by ordinary processes of reasoning and controlled by empirical methods, it does not follow that the numinous is non-rational, unless the term 'rational' be restricted to conceptual thinking.

As Otto admits, the beliefs and feelings involved in the numinous experience are "peculiar interpretations and valuations at first of perceptual data, and then—at a higher level—of posited objects and entities, which themselves no longer belong to the perceptual world, but are thought of as supplementing and transcending it".[1] In short, the numinous must become articulate to produce behaviour, and it is difficult to understand how it could be clothed with intelligible ideas if it were strictly non-rational. Nevertheless, he has called attention to an important element in the concept of the sacred by the emphasis he has laid on the peculiar character of religious awe and its distinction from what he calls 'natural feeling'. *Mana* is not exactly the equivalent of the 'numinous' since it is extraordinary power manifested in material objects or people, a kind of 'luck' or 'efficiency' which does not necessarily stimulate a sense of reverent regard and the awe-fulness or *mysterium tremendum*, so fundamental in the *religious* approach to the sacred. Anything that is unusual or great, effective or successful, may be thought to possess *mana* as something extra, whereas the numinous is an overpowering realization of transcendent holiness and daemonic dread. In this concept the uncanny, weird and uncommon acquire a new evaluation productive of a psychological response distinct from that of potency efficacious alike for good or evil, conducive to a receptive and submissive attitude which lies at the root of the religious response to sacredness.

The Sacred Drama

Religion, however, has emerged and developed under conditions sociological as well as psychological. In primitive society the deepest emotions and most heartfelt wants, hopes

[1] *Op. cit.*, page 117.

and fears are aroused within the context of the community, and find expression in concrete ritual situations and corporate acts of worship. Cult-legends may grow up around isolated figures, as at Bethel, but it has always been in the collective emotion of the sacred drama and the public ceremonies that the numinous has been most intensely realized, and exercised its influence as a social dynamic. Even among such a relatively cultured people as the Greeks, the stories of the gods and heroes were of little avail as a religious force by comparison with the dramatic rites held in the numinous atmosphere of the Hall of Initiation at Eleusis. There amid signs and circumstances calculated to produce an intense sense of awe and wonder, in which mysterious lights, sounds, plays and processions played their part, those who beheld these sacred sights and underwent the experience of initiation, emerged with a sense of having become reborn and renewed as the votaries of the goddess Demeter. In the wild ecstatic rites on mountain tops imported into Greece from Thrace, this rebirth was accomplished by frantic dancing, barbaric music and the free use of wine; but while the tumultuous worship of Dionysos remained an alien cult, it unquestionably aroused an intense religious fervour which passed as a wave over Greece in the sixth century B.C. If numinous and enthusiastic worship of this kind made no appeal to Greeks of the Homeric tradition, it aroused a longing in the hearts of those in whom it stirred a dormant desire to enter into communion with the divine, and to feel themselves lifted up from the temporal to the spiritual plane of being. These mysteries, it is true, were held in secret because the esoteric drama could only be beheld by the initiated, just as they alone could partake in the Dionysian revels, but, nevertheless, the cults were a closely knit corporation engaging in a dramatic act of corporate worship.

The word 'drama' is derived from the Greek *dromena*, 'the things done' in a ritual performance. When the sanctuary became a stage and the sacred actions 'the things acted,' 'dromena' was transformed into 'drama,' very much as the medieval Mystery Plays were derived from the great liturgical drama of the Mass. Indeed, these medieval plays grew out of the actions performed and the words spoken at the altar, and gradually became separate performances which eventually were secularized, though they never completely lost their ritual character either in ancient Greece or in medieval Christendom. Originally comedy was the ritual of life directed to making the crops grow and produce providential abundance ; tragedy was the ritual of death and decay alike in nature and in human existence. Taken together they portray the passage from life through death to life in greater abundance, be it in the processes of vegetation or in the earthly pilgrimage of man. So they give expression to the most fundamental religious emotion—the sense of dependence on a transcendent Providence—and the deepest human needs—the promotion and conservation of life, summed up, as Miss Jane Harrison says, in the ancient forumla, "out with famine, in with health and wealth".

"To live and to cause to live, to eat food and to beget children, these," in the words of Sir James Frazer, "were the primary wants of man in the past, and they will be the primary wants of man in the future so long as the world lasts. Other things may be added to enrich and beautify human life, but unless these wants are first satisfied, humanity itself must cease to exist. These two things, therefore, food and children, were what men chiefly sought to procure by the performance of magical rites for the regulation of the seasons." [1] Around them, from time immemorial, all the emotional evaluations and numinous experiences of primitive society have collected, and called into being sentiments on which the structure and constitution of society have depended for their stability by the influence they have exercised on its individual members in the establishment of an orderly social life. It is, in fact, because they touch the most vital concerns of the community as a whole that religion in general and ritual in particular have a sociological significance of the first importance.

The Sacred and Society

This has been emphasized by the French philosopher and

[1] *Golden Bough*, Part IV (Adonis, Attis, Osiris, Vol. I, page 5.

sociologist Emile Durkheim in his detailed analysis of the totemic organization among the native tribes of Australia. Religion, he thinks, arose in a collective form of experience based on the supposed relation between a human group and the supernatural symbol of society and its god. The god in the guise of a sacred species, animal or vegetable, or occasionally some inanimate object, known as the totem, is for Durkheim nothing less than the clan personified, and religion is "a unified system of beliefs and practices relative to sacred things, that is to say, things set apart and forbidden-beliefs and practices which unite into one single moral community called a Church all those who adhere to them".[1] The emblem of the clan (i.e. the totem) is the symbol of its corporate unity, and the rallying-point of the collective emotion. Consequently, it becomes the tribal god regarded as the expression of the forces by which the group imposes its authority upon its constituent members and so ensures the conditions of its own existence. Therefore, since the totem symbolizes the clan which is the real god, it collects around it the worship of the community. "In a general way a society," it is declared, "has all that is necessary to arouse the sensation of the divine in minds, merely by the power it has over them ; for to its members it is what a god is to its worshippers. The god and the clan can be nothing else than the clan itself." [2]

As an explanation of the origin of religion, apart from other considerations this very significant theory fails because it is based on the supposition that totemism represents the earliest form of religious belief and social organization. When in 1912 Durkheim published these conclusions in a volume entitled *Les Formes élementaires de la Vie religieuse* the evidence collected by Spencer and Gillen among the Central tribes of Australia (notably the Arunta or Aranda) lent considerable support to this very plausible hypothesis. But the tribal organization in this region, and the practice of totemism in general, are the product of a number of systems combined together into a composite whole which cannot be regarded

[1] *Elementary Forms of the Religious Life* (E.T., London, 1913), page 47.
[2] *Op. cit.*, pages 206ff.

as representing the simplest type of society as Durkheim and others have imagined. What the data reveal is not the way in which religion arose in the beginning but how it functions in the shaping and maintenance of the social and economic structure of the community.

Religion, however, is not merely a subjective reflection of society, a symbolic representation of its organization and group consciousness. The sense of the numinous, as we have seen, is aroused by an awareness of the *mysterium tremendum* in relation to natural phenomena quite as readily as to stimuli within society. Furthermore, the practice of religion is not confined to totemic seasonal ceremonies even among the Australian aborigines. On the contrary, the most numinous moments in the life of the black-fellow are those he experiences at the time of his initiation, when he is withdrawn from the community at large in the seclusion of the bush. Then it is, as he believes, that the spirit of some ancestor or departed relative appears to him in a dream, or under the guise of an animal, as his special protector, or guardian divinity. Such a manifestation is quite independent of "the individualized forms of collective forces" and "group effervescence" during periods of concentration. It is a personal and individual experience with no collective emotion to call it into being beyond the suggestion inculcated during the tribal ceremonies.

The Groundwork of Religion

Therefore, it would seem religion has not arisen solely from social organization or within a group context, however much it may function as an integral element in society. It is essentially a reaction to the numinous experienced in a great variety of circumstances and occurrences, some of which are individual and personal, others social and collective. The 'group theories' of Durkheim and those who have collaborated with him in the review known as *L'Année Sociologique*, retain too much of the mystic solidarity expounded by Comte in the first half of the last century, and lose sight of the part played by the interaction of individuals acting under the influence of a common environment, a common social inheritance and a similar psychological stimulus, rather than solely of that of collective consciousness and corporate sacred actions.

Whenever a man comes to the end of his tether and reaches an unbridgeable gap in his understanding, experience and control of human situations and natural events, he is liable to resort to magico-religious activities and techniques. These may take a variety of modes and forms of expression but the 'things done', or the words spoken, are individual acts and utterances, and proceed from personal emotions even though they may acquire a social and cultural value and a cosmological significance. The objects and occurrences which are regarded as sacred are mysterious and awe-inspiring in themselves, and so require a special ritual technique either to render them harmless or to derive from them power and strength and supernatural aid. It is their numinous character and attributes, not society or their social qualities, that lie at the root of the religious reaction. Without these aspects—the 'something extra' as Otto would say—they would not stimulate a religious response. Therefore, the sacred is distinguished from the profane not merely as 'things set apart and forbidden', or obligatory beliefs and practices imposed by society for its own ends and purposes, but because of its inherent numinous nature.

The Nature and Function of Magic

Thus, magic is differentiated from religion in that its virtue lies within its own traditionally prescribed rites, and, unlike *mana* or the numinous, it is not conceived as a mystic force distinct from physical power which "acts in all kinds of ways for good or evil". *Mana*, it is true, may sometimes work in and through human beings, as we have seen, but it is not confined to them and to a rigidly defined system of conditions, acts and observances. Magic, on the other hand, is never a universal force residing wherever the supernormal occurs. As Malinowski says, "it is literally and actually enshrined in man and can be handed on only from man to man, according to very strict rules of magical filiation, initiation and instruction".[1] It is never a manifestation of the numinous, and as an organized system of supercausation the magic art is distinct from the institutions of religion, however much the two traditions may converge and fuse in practice.

It would seem, therefore, that *mana* is not the common root from which both magic and religion have sprung, as Marett suggested. Nevertheless, it may be one of the links connecting the two disciplines since each arises in situations causing emotional stress, and functions as an aspect of the sacred. *Mana* is sacredness manipulated from without; magic is sacredness manipulated by means of rites and spells in which it operates through a human agent. Acting on the premise that 'like produces like', the magician in the exercise of his craft employs the technical equipment he has acquired by training and initiation. If he wants to produce rain he imitates the processes of nature in a series of symbolical actions, often accompanied by appropriate exclamations. But it is more than mimicry. The actors are animated by a great desire and to give utterance and visible expression to their intense emotion they reproduce the natural conditions (the sky, the clouds and the birds) in the belief that by so doing the end will be achieved. Probably it never occurs to them to inquire how the results are attained, whether by their own unaided acts or through the help of an intervening agent. It suffices that the ceremonies 'work'.

To ensure success, however, a good deal of specialized knowledge is required which often includes some acquaintance with meteorology, folk medicine (i.e. the use of herbs, poisons, leechcraft, etc.), trephining and ligatures, together with real psychic gifts which are developed by training. In the healing of disease a preliminary diagnosis is usually made to determine the nature of the complaint. Appropriate gestures, such as sucking violently at the affected spot to extract a bone, or some other malignant object, are adopted, and success depends largely on the suggestibility of the patient. In serious cases, other practitioners may be called upon to assist, or the services of a renowned medicine man may be

[1] *Science, Religion and Reality* (London, 1926), page 71.

sought whose reputation will greatly heighten the susceptibility of the patient ; a consideration that is doubtless not wholly without significance in more advanced methods of the application of medical skill. But in primitive states of culture, apart from prestige, the great healer is supposed to be in possession of more potent 'medicine' calculated to counteract evil magic perpetuated by a rival exercising the black art. Therefore, if he projects some of his own sacred stones into the patient they will be correspondingly effective, while his utterances and invocations will give expression to the same emotion as efficacious spells which cannot be thwarted. But since disease and death normally are attributed to supernatural causes, should the operation fail in the end it will be explained in terms of a superior counter-magical efficiency. This will be bad for the reputation of the local practitioner but it does not weaken belief in the profession as a whole, and the memory of the failure is soon wiped out by subsequent successes.

In addition to the art of healing, medicine-men are employed in love-making, the control of the weather, the chase, the growth of crops, and in fact in almost any undertaking where super-causation is sought to bring about desired results outside the sphere in which man has the rational mastery of his circumstances. At the point where his own natural knowledge and technical abilities cease to operate, magic or religion, or a combination of both disciplines, comes into force. Therefore, the exercise of supernatural efficacy is regarded as absolutely indispensable to the welfare of the community, even though it may be abused and put to sinister uses, as in the case of black magic. Thus, if sickness is due to malignant agencies made operative by spell or rite, magic is at once illicit in producing the disease and licit in effecting the cure. Furthermore, the same person is capable of employing his powers either to save life or to kill, to heal or to destroy. It is a question of intention, but whether a bone is sung over and pointed at a victim to wound and slay him, or extracted to effect the cure, the distinction is not between magic and religion, as Jevons suggested, but between two aspects of the same kind of traffic with the supernatural.

Thus, the medicine-man may be either a worker of white magic, when he exercises his office for the well-being of mankind, or he may descend to the black art when he engages in nefarious practices. In the former capacity his rites are frequently performed in public, as in the case of rain-making. But this is not a universal rule since love-magic, for instance, though not vicious, is usually a clandestine affair.

Magic and Religion

Taken as a whole magic cannot be distinguished from religion in terms of good and evil intentions, of publicity and secrecy, or by its effects on society and the individual. The fundamental differentiation lies rather in the nature of the approach to and the control of the sacred order and its agencies. Religion presupposes a reverential attitude to the numinous in its various aspects which finds expression in worship, conciliation and abasement. Magic is essentially practical, consisting of precisely prescribed ritual acts and utterances to attain specific ends by their own inherent efficacy. Whether or not spirits, ancestors or even gods lurk in the background, magic always involves the knowledge and use of spells and formulæ which constitute the essential controlling element in the performances as the dramatic form of some emotion.

Again, magic, like religion and *mana*, arises out of a sense of frustration, a realisation of an inability to meet critical and inexplicable situations, to interpret the meaning of signs and wonders, or by natural means to ward off "the slings and arrows of outrageous fortune". Since they all represent the same emotional attitude to the sacred, notwithstanding these individual peculiarities and distinguishing features, in practice they tend to converge. In most cases there is no conscious process of thinking. In short, primitive man "dances out his religion," manipulates his magic and utilizes his *mana* for specific purposes without analysing his actions or theorizing about his methods.

Thus, the medicine-man sometimes resorts to spells and charms to heal his patient or injure his victim, to arouse love or hate, to bring rain, promote fertility or secure good hunting and fishing. He may then be described as a magician. But he has also other functions which differentiate him from the worker of magic pure and simple, and bring him into closer relations with the prophet and the priest. He may owe his supernormal power to the spirits with whom he is *en rapport* and then he may be able to do nothing of himself except it be given him from the higher powers. The rain-maker, the seer, the diviner and the spirit-medium, it is true, do not exercise priestly functions in the sense of ministering at an altar or serving a sanctuary in a sacerdotal capacity. But the line of demarcation wears thin when an individual acts as the official representative of transcendental powers, or is regarded as a sacred or semi-divine person. Similarly, the shaman who drums and dances himself into an ecstasy in order to gain supernormal wisdom and knowledge, is well on his way to the prophetic office. Unlike the priest in whom supernatural power is fixed by virtue of his ordination, which has conferred upon him in perpetuity a certain 'character', the prophet and shaman tend to become sporadically god or spirit-possessed like Saul on his return from his search for the asses (I Sam., x, 10f., cf. xix, 18ff.), and to display highly emotional symptoms in attaining communion with the spirit-world.

So far from the priest being the lineal descendant of the magician, as Frazer has suggested, and religion the sequel of ineffective magic, in a given rite incantations and prayers, imitative enchantments and supplications and mediatorial offerings, often are so intermingled in bewildering confusion that an observer is at a loss to know into what theoretical category to place either the ceremony or the officiants. Separated from their context, many of the elements would be classified as magical in their nature and efficacy, but if the cultus is primarily an expression of a numinous attitude of mind towards the sacred, outside the coercive control of man, it is essentially a religious institution even though there may be a constraining element in some of the actions performed. In short, priests, medicine-men, rain-makers, shamans, diviners and the like in primitive society cannot be placed in watertight compartments labelled magic or religion and arranged in chronological sequence as the antecedents or descendants of each other. It is out of a fluid state in which the two approaches to the sacred are in solution that in process of time more or less distinct traditions have crystallized, each having its own characteristics. In appearance and in practice the disciplines often have been indistinguishable because to the primitive mind clear cut differentiations are not perceptible in the stress and strain of the struggle for existence and the effort to gain the mastery of a complex and overpowering environment, always demanding the aid and intervention of supernatural forces and powers, however these may be conceived and employed.

BIBLIOGRAPHY

Castigliani, A. *Adventures of the Mind*. London, 1947.

Codrington, R. H. *The Melanesians ; Studies in their Anthropology and Folk-Lore*. Oxford, 1891.

Durkheim, E. *The Elementary Forms of the Religious Life*. Eng. Trans. New York, 1913.

Frazer, J. G. *The Golden Bough*. Vol. I. The Magic Art. Pt. I. London, 1917.

Harrison, J. *Prolegomena to the Study of Greek Religion*. Cambridge, 1922. *Ancient Art and Ritual*. London, 1913.

Hewitt, J. N. B. "Orenda and a Definition of Religion" in *The American Anthropologist*. New Series. IV. 1902. pp. 102ff.

James, E. O. *Primitive Ritual and Belief*. London, 1917. *Comparative Religion*. London, 1938.

Jevons, F. B. *Introduction to the History of Religion*. London, 1896.

Malinowski, B. *The Foundations of Faith and Morals*. Oxford, 1936. "Magic, Science and Religion" in *Science, Religion and Reality*. London, 1926.

Marett, R. R. *The Threshold of Religion*. London, 1914.

Murphy, J. *Primitive Man : his essential Quest*. Oxford, 1927.

Otto, R. *The Idea of the Holy*. Eng. Trans. 1928.

Webb, C. C. J. *Group Theories of Religion and the Individual*. London, 1916.

Westermarck, E. *Ritual and Belief in Morocco*. Vol. I. London, 1926.

CHAPTER II

PROVIDENCE

We pass now from the generalized notion of the sacred, which appears to lie at the root of both religion and magic, marked off from the profane as an order of super-causation, to the more particularized concrete interpretations and valuations of cult and belief. In this region of the super-sensible and super-normal there are a jumble of phenomena—gods, ghosts, spirits, totems, ancestors and so on—which find expression in animatism, animism, totemism, ancestor-worship, the cult of the dead and theism, all reacting one on the other. To reduce this confusion to something approaching order is by no means easy, and in the process, as we have seen, modern scientific observers and theorists are liable to isolate as distinct categories, systems, concepts, and disciplines, beliefs and practices that the primitive mind is incapable of keeping asunder. There are, however, certain fundamental realities which stand out clearly even in the confused state of primitive mentality concerning matters which constitute focal points, such as beliefs about the conservation and promotion of life, centring in the food quest, conception, sex, marriage, birth, adolescence and death. Around these basic elements a ritual organization has developed which has had profound and far-reaching sociological repercussions in the maintenance of human existence and the stabilization of society.

The Idea of Providence

Food and children being the primary needs of every community these two essential requirements have become the tokens of the beneficence of the world which may be summed up in our term *Providence*. It is this notion of providential bounty that represents the concrete universal good. Upon it man is dependent for his sustenance, well-being and for the continuance of the race. The institutions of religion are the means by which communion with and in beneficent abundance is secured, and the evil of want and sterility is annulled. Therefore, a reverent attitude has to be adopted towards the mysterious forces of nutrition and propagation since they are objects of religious regard and centres of emotional interest and concern. To primitive man, as Malinowski has said, "nature is his living larder" and prior to the discovery of methods of cultivating the soil and domesticating animals, when he lives a precarious existence relying for his food supply mainly on the chase and such edible fruits, roots and berries as can be collected, the animal and vegetable species which form his stable diet are the personification of Providence—the mysterious bounty of nature in which he lives day by day.

Thus, in primitive society, the whole process of securing and consuming food is invested with a supernatural significance of its own which renders it sacred and so not to be lightly approached. The natural function of eating becomes a participation in the fruits of providential beneficence involving an organized ritual technique approved by society for dealing with a critical aspect of human life, and culminating very often in a sacramental meal to establish a vital bond between man and the sacred source of his means of subsistence (i.e. Providence). By sharing in food sacramentally with the powers to which he looks for his daily supplies, the savage shares with them in the bounty of his Providence and makes some amends for the painful necessity of destroying species with which he is in a sacred relationship.

Guardian Spirits

The animals being his elder brothers, stronger and wiser than himself, differing from him in bodily form but animated by the same life principle, or soul-substance, to kill them appears in the light of slaying a kinsman. Among the Arunta tribes of Central Australia, for instance, each human being is regarded as the incarnation of an ancestor, or mythical animal, from which he derived his name and descent and with which he and the rest of the members of his clan stand in this peculiar relationship as the source of their life. Similarly, in North America supernatural power is thought by some of the Indian tribes to reside in certain animals which appear to youths at the time of their initiation. Sometimes a man retires in seclusion to the top of a mountain, or to an island in a lake, or any unfrequented spot, where he remains without food until the creature manifests itself in a vision as his secret helper, or *nagual*, and gives him the guidance he is seeking. An initiate destined to be a warrior will have a vision of an eagle or a bear, a serpent will appear to the future medicine-man, a wolf to the hunter. To complete the bond a portion of the nagual is worn about his person as an embodiment of its soul-substance. Sometimes, as among the Déné, a representative of the animal is painted in vermilion on prominent rocks in the most frequented places.[1]

Since the tutelary or guardian spirit is the link which connects man with the invisible world and the means of communing with the beneficent powers of Providence, to kill and eat animals so closely akin to himself is an anomaly. Yet willy nilly he is compelled to hunt in order to live, and when the sources of supply are limited, he may be driven to seek his food among the sacred species, even when the particular guardian of an individual is strictly taboo to the person in question. Among the Ainu of Japan the bear is sacrosanct and regarded as an ancestor, yet by force of circumstances they are compelled to hunt it whenever possible. To make amends for the painful necessity of killing a creature which is at once a providential source of the food supply and a kinsman, the victim is admired, thanked and venerated after a 'kill'. Furthermore, a cub is caught at birth and suckled by a woman to establish a sort of 'milk brotherhood' with the sacred species. It is then slain ceremonially at a solemn festival after due apology ; prayers are addressed to it and the flesh is eaten sacramentally. Sometimes the blood

[1]G. Morice, *Proceedings of the Canadian Institute* (Toronto, 1889), 3rd Series, Vol. VII, page 161.

is drunk warm that the courage and other virtues it possesses may be imbibed.[1]

In Alaska and North-eastern Siberia an animal is seldom killed without some apology and the bear is singled out for a special festival only because it is the principal source of the food supply. The skulls of foxes are also set up on posts outside the huts as well as those of bears, and addressed as 'precious divinities,' though a milk tribute is not levied on the tribal mothers as among the Ainu. An individual animal, however, is killed and eaten ritually in order that the common life of the group may be reinforced and the daily slaughter required by human necessities is compounded for by a ceremonial gesture of good feeling and universal regret for a practical need.

Totemism

In these ceremonies the bear hardly fulfils the place and function of a totem, in the usual sense in which this term is applied to a particular sacred species or natural object with which a group of human beings believe themselves to stand in a peculiarly exclusive relationship of kinship and descent, and from which the clan derives its name. In Australia, Melanesia and Africa the prohibition to kill and eat the eponymous ancestor is strictly observed, and in several Bantu languages the word 'totem' means 'the forbidden thing'. In America the taboo is much less prominent, but the complete absence of any restrictions on the hunting and eating of bears among the Ainu and Siberian tribes, or indeed of any mystic relationship between the species and the hunters, seems to rule out a totemic interpretation of the cult. Bears are venerated because they are the most prominent expression of providential bounty and, therefore, it behoves the people who are so dependent upon them for their food supply to keep on friendly and beneficial relations with them. The apologies for killing, the kindly treatment of the cub and its suckling by the women, are directed to this end—a token of good will and an acknowledgment of the blessings so lavishly bestowed upon them by a generous Providence.

[1] Batchelor, *The Ainu and their Folk-lore* (London, 1910), page 471ff.

In Central Australia, on the other hand, a highly complicated organization has developed on a definitely totemic basis in which elaborate ceremonies are performed by each of the clans for the purpose of making the animals, birds, plants and insects which figure as totems increase and multiply. Thus, before the rains begin when the land is arid a group of men belonging to the witchetty grub totemic clan assemble at Emily Gap in the Arunta country—a sacred spot long associated with the totemic ancestors and decorated with drawings of this particular totem (the witchetty grub). After observing a rigid fast and divesting themselves of clothing and decorations, they follow their leader, with little twigs of the Udniringa bush in their hands, to a particular spot known as *Ilthuran oknira*, high up on the western wall of the Gap. The entire district is full of sacred lore concerning the exploits of the ancestors, as will be shown later,[1] and almost every natural object is connected with some traditional site designed to fulfil a sociological function. Consequently, everything has to be done during the Intichiuma ceremony strictly in accord with the carefully defined practice, otherwise the efficacy will be impeded.

Having arrived at a shallow cave in which is a large block of quartzite representing the adult witchetty grub (*maegwa*), surrounded by smaller stones (*churinga unchima*) depicting its eggs, the leader taps the *maegwa* with his small *pitchi*, or wooden vessel corresponding to the trough in which the culture hero Intwailinka carried his store of spirits and bull-roarers in the Alcheringa. Each man then strikes it with his twigs while songs are sung invoking the grub to lay eggs. The tappings over, the head man strikes all his companions on their stomachs with one of the *churinga unchima* saying, "You have eaten much food". This ceremony is repeated on the way back to the camp when halts are made at various sacred holes in the hillside where stones representing the chrysalis state of the totem have been deposited. After each man's stomach has been rubbed again with a stone called *churinga uchaqua* representing the chrysalis stage of the grub, to the accompaniment of the same chant, about a mile from

[1] cf. Chapter VII, pp.

the final destination they decorate themselves with the totemic designs, head bands, hair strings, feathers and nose-bones. Meanwhile the old men who were left behind in the camp have constructed a long narrow *wurley* or hut, during their absence, to represent the chrysalis from which the grub emerges. Surrounded by the men and women of other moieties of the tribe, the party on their return wriggle in and out of the hut singing of the insect in its various stages, and of the ancestral stones recently visited. Not until this has been done are they permitted to break their fast. Then food and water are brought to them by the old men who built the *wurley*. This they consume in the hut and at dusk sit outside as they sing of the witchetty grub till daybreak. Then the ceremony is brought to an abrupt end with the words, "our Intichiuma is finished, the *Mulganuka*[1] must have these things or else our Intichiuma would not be successful, and some harm would happen to us". They all reply, "yes, yes, certainly". The ornaments are handed over to the men of the other moiety, the designs are removed from the bodies of the performers, who thereupon return to their respective camps.[2]

The purpose of the rites is to increase the supply of the insects for the benefit of the whole community. The mythological geographical setting, the actions performed and the words spoken do not admit of any other interpretation. When it is said that the men who are still fasting have eaten much food, the reference must be to the creation of plenty by anticipation rather than to the actual consumption of the sacred species. Indeed, the witchetty grub may be eaten only sparingly by the members of the totem at any time, and then not until the sacred food has been desacralized by a kind of sacramental meal, *after Intichiuma* when it is plentiful. Then supplies are gathered, cooked and stored away in *pitchis*. In due course they are taken to the men's camp where the leader grinds up their contents between stones. He and the other men of the totem eat a little and distribute what remains to those who do not belong to the totem, very

[1] i.e., Men of the other moiety.

[2] *Native Tribes of Central Australia*, pages 170ff.

much as at the end of the Intichiuma. The ornaments of the ritual party are given to the men of the other moiety and on this we are told the success of the rites depends.[1] Therefore, it is clearly the duty of each group to make its contribution toward the food supply of the entire community by the due performance of the rites which are believed to promote the fertility of its own totemic species, but from the beneficent results of which it derives little or no benefit.

Analogous ceremonies occur in the neighbouring tribes, and in all cases the totem is relatively taboo to the performers, who only eat it as a kind of sacramental meal on the first-fruits of their own labours in its ritual production. Having contributed to its increase and vitality, they in their turn desire to share in the providential bounty they have in a measure supplied. So they partake of the sacred food in a becomingly ritualistic, apologetic and abstemious manner, like the Ainu, in order that the natural function of eating may be consecrated to a spiritual meaning and purpose. Thus, when an Intichiuma ceremony is to be performed in the Undiara kangaroo totem, the men proceed to the foot of a hill on the slope of which two blocks of stone project, one above the other. One of these stones is supposed to represent a male kangaroo, the other a female kangaroo. The head man of the clan with a man who is in the relation of maternal uncle to him climbs up to the two blocks and rubs them with a stone. They then repair to a rocky ledge thought to be haunted by the spirits of ancestral kangaroos and paint it with stripes of red and white to indicate the red fur and white bones of the kangaroo. When this has been done a number of the young men sit on the top of the ledge while the men below sing of the *increase* of the kangaroos. To drive out in all directions the spirit-parts of the species, the men open veins in their arms and allow the blood to stream on to and over the ledge of the sacred stone which marks the spot where a celebrated kangaroo in the Alcheringa, or Golden Age, went down into the earth leaving his spirit in the boulder that arose to indicate the spot. The young men then go and hunt kangaroos and bring back their spoils

[1] *Op. cit.*, pages 203ff.

to the camp. The leader and the old men eat a little of the flesh of the animal and anoint with its fat the bodies of those who took part in the Intichiuma. This done the meat is divided among them all, and they spend the night in dancing and singing songs relating to the exploits of the Alcheringa ancestors. The sacred species may then be eaten sparingly.[1]

Here, again, as in the witchetty grub ceremonies, the purpose of the rite is to maintain and increase the food supply and by so doing to establish a mystic covenant or communion with a beneficent Providence, symbolized by the supernatural ally or totem. By the ritual shedding of blood a vital bond is ratified and sealed in the common soul-substance of man and the sacred species. Life is given to promote and conserve life and to consolidate the sacramental relationship on which the continuance and well-being of the community depend. Natural means of hunting and collecting animals, plants and insects not sufficing to meet every emergency, magico-religious methods have to be employed to ensure an adequate food supply and to maintain a correct attitude towards the source of beneficence. Furthermore, as Dr. Marett has remarked, "it looks rather as if the point of so scrupulous an eating were to express an apology for a none too scrupulous killing".[2]

Providence and Propagation

This will to live which finds an outlet in the ritual control of the means of subsistence has its counterpart in an intense desire for children. Therefore, as propagation stands beside nutrition as the foremost vital concern of the human race, marriage and the family are intimately connected with the notion of providential bounty. If primitive folk are not quite as ignorant of the facts of generation as has been suggested by many observers, for a number of reasons, the function of the father has tended to become obscured in the process of procreation. While analogies must have been drawn from animal generative behaviour by hunters familiar with the life and habits of nature (notwithstanding the fact that Malinowski

[1] *Op. cit.*, pages 204f.

[2] *Sacraments of Simple Folk* (Oxford, 1933), page 30.

denies the existence of such knowledge among the Trobriand islanders), the idea of the dual origin of body and soul has obscured the significance of the sex act in human intercourse. Thus, as late as the Middle Ages there was much speculation respecting the relation of generation to the origin of the soul as a divine gift. Consequently, when in primitive society it is supposed that children are the reincarnation of the spirit-part of a totemic ancestor, and many matings occur at times of orgiastic licence and periodic ceremonial promiscuity, a state of uncertainty must exist about individual paternity. That copulation has been known to be an integral part of the process of generation since at least the middle of the Old Stone Age is clear from the widespread and continuous use of sexual symbolism in the promotion of fertility, but it is not improbable that, as in Melanesia to-day, the function of the male has been considered to be that of opening the way for the entrance of the embryo into the woman from some transcendental source, and so is only very indirectly concerned with the birth of a particular child from a single father.

In Australia, the Central and Northern tribes believe that spirit-children pass into women of the right totem at spots marked by natural features associated with the ancestors who are thought to have deposited embryos there in the Dream Time, or Alcheringa, when they wandered about on the earth. There they await rebirth by entering a potential mother through the navel, or by running up her legs when she is wading in a neighbouring lagoon, or standing in a river near a particular gum tree. If she stoops to drink the water, one of the sprites may jump into her mouth, and the same may happen when she is eating certain kinds of food. Thus, in this area it appears that the birth of children bears no direct relation to sexual intercourse, the centre of interest, so far as offspring are concerned, being the ingress of the incarnated spirit from the transcendental world. And this event is connected with the symptoms of pregnancy and quickening rather than with the initial act of begetting. Wherever she happens to be when she first becomes conscious of her condition, there she thinks the spirit-child has entered her, and as the countryside is studded with sacred places and objects, she is not at a loss to find a suitable site for the abode of her embryo. The Australian theory of generation, however, has every appearance of being a highly artificial system which doubtless has undergone very considerable modification in the process of its development. Totemism, in fact, is far too complicated a system to represent the primeval organization of human society, and in its Australian form it seems to have combined a mode of social grouping with religious beliefs about Providence and food, reincarnation and marriage, the common element being the transcendental control of fecundity and its practical application to every day life in a given locality.

If, however, the Australian evidence does not throw much light on the more rudimentary conceptions of paternity among peoples in a primitive state of culture, it at least shows that human birth is regarded as an intervention of Providence. Being a spirit-child emanating from the never-dying spirit of the ancestral stock, its entry into the world through the mother is independent of human generation, notwithstanding a remote causal connexion with sexual intercourse as a preparation for the reception of the embryo into the womb. From the moment of quickening the incarnated spirit is a denizen from the 'other world', associated with the totem or the ancestors. At birth the infant is either an old soul rejuvenated in a new body or a spirit-child of the ancestral stock. Thus, totemism is an institution through which a social group establishes an intimate relation with a species of animal or plant, or an object or class of objects, accounted as its ancestor. The totem is virtually a reservoir for the potency of the group and from it is drawn the continuous life of the community through a process of reincarnation. When society is organized on this basis, the sacred ally is the centre around which the social and religious structure revolves. Nevertheless, behind the clan is the family, and the development would seem to have been from this social unit to the group.

Marriage and the Family

Before a clan organization arose and assumed a totemic structure, probably taboos collected around the mother (either actual or expectant) as the productive centre, to protect her at a critical juncture in her career, and to prevent sexual disturbance in the household. Whatever uncertainties there may have been about paternity and the precise relation of intercourse between husband and wife and the birth of children, the fact of motherhood is beyond any possibility of doubt. Therefore, around the mother and the sanctity of her blood all the mysterious forces associated with the entry into the world of a new member of the family have collected. She is the self-sufficing source of life so far as this world is concerned, and behind her is the ultimate transcendental order whence springs all vitality, using her as its instrument, and endowing her with an inherent sanctity compelling respectful avoidance or reverential approach. So around her the two fundamental taboos have gathered : (1) the horror of shedding the blood of a kinsman, and (2) the dread of incest.

If, however, the relationship between mother and child as the starting-point of the family lies at the base of the emotional development upon which society has been built, communal marriage and a communal nursery (such as the theory of primitive promiscuity urged by McLennan, Morgan and Briffault, presupposes) do not fulfil either the sociological conditions of human culture or the biological and psychological requirements of the human organism. The home rather than the herd is the nucleus of society and the mother is the instrument of Providence as the centre and source of the family. Hence the elaborate regulations safeguarding marriage and a healthy and harmonious home life, enforced by the sanctions of religion, as an essential element in the maintenance of the social order as a whole.

Moreover, while matriarchal conditions in which the husband often occupies a subordinate position as a rather casual visitor, are of common occurrence they are not universal. On the contrary, very simple folk like the Pygmies of Central Africa tend to be monogamous, a man and woman living together in their own hut with their offspring, very much as the higher monkeys and apes usually live in families consisting of father, mother and their young. "There is not a shred of genuine evidence," as Westermarck says, "for the notion that promiscuity ever formed a general stage in the history of mankind,"[1] and Elliot Smith is correct in regarding the family as "the grouping invariably formed in the absence of an alien influence" to give expression to man's innate tendencies.[2] Indeed, the sentiments underlying the development of culture can only be fostered within a family organization which makes it possible for the young to be nurtured for a prolonged period.

The urge of life from within and the struggle for existence from without have joined forces in an endeavour to promote and preserve fecundity, and the beginning of culture implies the repression of anti-social instincts. This is accomplished by the institution of the family in which a vital tension is created involving moral effort and the subordination of individual desires to the common good. The function of religion in this process is to preserve intact the family organization by surrounding it with supernatural sanctions and taboos designed to prevent marital or sexual relationships which are liable to be destructive of the psychological foundations and harmony of the home. It is here that the providential control of propagation is introduced to safeguard and stabilize the unit of society at its most vital point by bringing it within the tribal ritual organization.

Since the process of begetting and giving birth is part of the complex system of supercausation requiring a supernatural approach, the ritual status of the mother as the reproductive centre of the home has to be protected by taboos like all other providential interventions. Therefore, around her has collected all the mysterious forces associated with fertility comparable to those connected with the food supply, which later were personified in the seasonal drama in terms of human generation. In short, in feeding and breeding, nutrition and nurture, the first inklings of Providence may be discerned as part of a sacred order regulated by supernatural sanctions and magico-religious rites of a sacramental character. But human well-being necessitated an expanding

[1] *History of Human Marriage* (London, 1921), Vol. I, page 336.
[2] *Human History* (London, 1930), page 234.

social and economic organization and as growth of language facilitated the exchange of ideas, so collective enterprise promoted the community spirit compelling men to evolve a social structure adequate to the needs of a developing society, but still grounded in the 'other world'.

Providence and the Divine Kingship

The transition from hunting, fishing and collecting food to the cultivation of the soil and the domestication of animals at the dawn of civilization had a profound effect upon the conception of Providence. The ritual control of fertility and food production now came to be concentrated upon the cultivation of crops and rearing of flocks and herds. Under this new economy a social structure emerged which was unified and consolidated in and around the august figure of the divine king, who was believed to be the incarnation of the gods upon whose beneficent offices the community depended for its well-being. Exactly how mighty chiefs, powerful medicine-men, great benefactors and other important functionaries in the food-gathering tribes assumed their new position and acquired this royal status is a matter of conjecture about which expert opinion is still undecided. But it is clear that behind the imposing figure of the Egyptian Pharaoh there stands the shadow of a humbler person who reigned by virtue of the supernatural power he wielded over the processes of nature and of all life. Pharaoh, in fact, was accredited with almost exactly the same functions assigned to these more primitive divine kings who control the weather, make women and cattle fruitful and foretell the future by divination.

Thus, in Ancient Egypt where cereal cultivation appears to have begun in some of the Fayum settlements and those of Tasa and Badari between 5500 and 4500 B.C., the ruler was regarded as the source of the prosperity of the Nile valley and the living epitome of all that is divine. He was, in short, the earthly embodiment of the primitive notion of Providence. In his complex personality he summed up the attributes of all the gods he embodied, presumably because ultimately for the Egyptians they were actually a plurality in unity.

When the Pharaoh is first encountered in the Egyptian texts he is represented as of divine origin and descent, whether it be as the son of the Sun-god or in the guise of Horus, the living king, and so equated at his death also with the culture hero Osiris. He is said to "illuminate the Two lands (i.e. Upper and Lower Egypt) more than the sun-disk. He makes the Two Lands green more than a great Nile; he hath filled the Two Lands with strength". He is "the one creating that which is"; "the Begetter, who causes the people to be". Having himself been conceived through the incestuous union of the reigning monarch with his sister to ensure the divine descent of the heir to the throne, he daily renewed his divinity in the so-called Toilet Ceremonies he performed in the House of the Morning. Moreover, at stated intervals, estimated at thirty years, he underwent a symbolic death and resurrection in union with the dead king Osiris whom he also impersonated.

This is significant because the Egyptians believed that Osiris was the king who reigned over Egypt in prehistoric times, taught the secrets of agriculture, and after a prosperous rule was either slain or drowned through the treachery of his brother Set. The queen Isis, however, conceived a son named Horus after the death of Osiris by hovering over the body of her dead husband; and it was he who eventually avenged the murder of his father and restored him to life. Therefore, Osiris became, as it were, the embodiment of dead kingship while the living king was equated with Horus. It was this myth which found ritual expression in the periodic renewal rites known as the Sed-festival, as well as in the Spring and Harvest festivals, in which the king was the principal officiant.

Behind this ancient story and its enactment there may lurk the widespread custom, to which Frazer has called attention, of putting divine kings to death when they begin to show signs of senility or loss of vigour. This extreme practice has been closely associated with the belief that because the monarch is the dynamic centre of vitality he controls the weather, the growth of the crops and the processes of reproduction, so that the failure of his own generative powers must have a reciprocal effect in men, animals and plants. To prevent a general decline in fecundity he is killed either after he has reigned for a limited period, or as soon as any indication is given of failing virility.

It is significant that in Egyptian tradition Osiris is represented in the guise of the founder of civilization in the Nile valley, and it is conceivable that he really was an enlightened king who reigned in the Delta and was largely responsible for the introduction of agriculture. He may also have been the first person to cut canals for the purpose of irrigating the land. In any case, in the mind of the dynastic Egyptians he was very intimately connected with vegetation and the fructifying waters of the Nile. Therefore, as an object of worship he was always represented as the *dead* king exercising his life-giving functions through his posthumous son, Horus.

The Sacrifice of the Divine King

In primitive agricultural tribes the custom of killing the king frequently has undergone some modification along the lines indicated by the Sed-festival of Ancient Egypt. Sometimes a member of the royal family such as the eldest son, or a male descendant, has been substituted for the reigning monarch, but another practice has been to chose a prisoner of war, or some other commoner, to play the fatal rôle for a year, and then pay the supreme penalty of his office. Thus, among the Aztecs in Mexico, where no less than two thousand victims, it has been estimated, were immolated annually to promote the growth of the maize, at the Annual Festival held when the sun was at its height in April, a virile young prisoner of war in royal estate was led forth to his doom. For a year he had lived in the temple waited on by nobles, served as a prince and treated as a god when he appeared in the streets. He consorted with four brides known respectively as the goddess of flowers, the goddess of the young maize, the goddess of "our mother among the water", and the goddess of salt, and when the destined day arrived he bade farewell to his wives and was led to a lonely pyramidal temple where his heart was extracted and offered to the Sun-god. Immediately the sacrifice had been made his successor was invested with the status for the next year, so that the substitute for the king was as it were perpetually in office. *Le roi est mort, vive le roi.* During the last five days of the 'reign' of the mock sovereign, the real king remained quiescent in the seclusion of his palace undergoing a kind of ritual death while the entire court clustered round his substitute.[1]

Human sacrifice, however, represents only a temporary phase in the history of religion which reaches its height in the vegetation ritual of Mexico. It belongs essentially to semi-civilized peoples engaged in the cultivation of the soil, and while, as we shall see when the institution of sacrifice is considered in greater detail in a later chapter,[2] it survived among the ancient urban civilizations from the Near East to Central America, it was modified by ritual substitutes of which the Sed-festival in Egypt may be an example. The purpose of the rite was to secure the bountiful gifts of Providence through a fresh outpouring of divine life inherent in the royal victim or his surrogate. To this end the offering has been made usually and most appropriately at the seasonal changes in the year when the growth of the crops are in jeopardy, and vital energy is in urgent need of renewal.

The king in agricultural society taking the place of the totem in a food-gathering economy, is the victim in person or by substitute because he is the symbol of Providence, and by virtue of his office as the dynamic centre of vitality he becomes both priest and victim offering himself on behalf of his people. Ideally he dies that they may live. In practice a deputy may take his place at the altar, or he may undergo a ceremonial death and revival as when the Pharaoh in Ancient Egypt assumed the costume and insignia of Osiris to secure a new lease of life and rejuvenescence of his divine energies through thus identifying himself with the dead hero

[1] B. de Sahagun, *Histoire Générale des choses de la Nouvelle Espagne* (Paris, 1880), pages 61ff . . . 96ff.

[2] cf. Chapter IV, pages 83ff.

who was resuscitated by Horus and Isis. That this was the purpose of the ritual seems probable since in the inscriptions of Abydos it is recorded that after the festival the king was addressed as follows: "Thou beginnest thy renewal, beginnest to flourish again like the infant god of the Moon, thou art young again year by year, like Nun at the beginning of the ages, thou art reborn by renewing thy festival of *Sed*".[1] But whatever may have been the significance of this very ancient Egyptian rite, in primitive agricultural society in dying to live the king was regarded as the earthly representative and incarnation of Providence embodying in his person the dynamic forces and powers by which life is retained, renewed and bestowed henceforth in greater abundance.

BIBLIOGRAPHY

Batchelor, J. *The Ainu and their Folklore*. London, 1901.

Breasted, J. H. *Religion and Thought in Ancient Egypt*. London, 1912.

Briffault, R. *The Mothers*. London, 1927. Vol. I–III.

Crawley, A. E. *The Mystic Rose*. New Edition by T. Besterman. London, 1927.

Elkin, A. P. *The Australian Aborigines*. Sydney and London, 1938.

Frazer, J. G. *Early History of Kingship*. London, 1905. *The Golden Bough*. Pt. IV. The Dying God. · London, 1914.

Harrison, J. *Ancient Art and Ritual*. London, 1913.

Hartland, S. *Primitive Paternity*. London, 1909-10.

Im Thurn, E. F. *Among the Indians of Guiana*. London, 1883.

Hocart, A. M. *Kingship*. Oxford, 1927.

Malinowski, B. *Sex and Repression in Savage Society*. London, 1927. *The Father in Primitive Psychology*. London, 1927.

Marett, R. R. *Sacraments of Simple Folk*. Oxford, 1933.

Seligman, C. G. *Egypt and Negro Africa*. London, 1934.

Spencer, B., and Gillen, F. J. *Native Tribes of Central Australia*. London, 1899. *The Arunta*. London, 1927.

Westermarck, E. *History of Human Marriage*. Vols. I–III. London, 1921. *Three Essays on Sex and Marriage*. London, 1934.

[1] Moret, *Du caractère Religieux de la royauté Pharaonique* (Paris, 1902), page 256.

CHAPTER III

SPIRITS, ANCESTORS AND GODS

WHEN the human mind began to form mental concepts and ideas corresponding to abstract terms attempts were made, it would seem, to rationalize the ritual organization that had grown up around the fundamental realities and necessities of existence which we have grouped together under the general heading of 'Providence'. It is at this point in the development of religion that animistic beliefs in spiritual beings, ghosts of the dead, ancestors and individualized divinities become differentiated as integral parts of a coherent whole, viz., of the order of the sacred. Actions and utterances expressing the inmost desires and emotions of the human heart are abstracted and interpreted in relation to mythical beings and particular spirits associated with special topographical features, natural species, cosmic phenomena and extraordinary events which are believed to control for good or ill human destinies and the course of nature. Supernatural potency now acquires *will* and lives a life of its own comparable to, though transcending, human existence.

The Animistic interpretation of Nature

Thus, in the latter part of the last century it was thought that the primitive mind peopled the universe with a multiplicity of spirits, souls or wills inhabiting "every rock and hill, every tree and flower, every brook and river, every breeze that blew, and every cloud that flecked with silvery white the blue expanse of heaven". From this general animation of nature, so vividly described by Frazer, in course of time a god of the woods, it was suggested, was substituted for the spirits of the individual trees, and a single god of the winds took the place of the animistic personifications of all the winds, each with his distinct character and features. But "the instinctive craving of the mind for simplification and unification of its ideas" was supposed to have produced a further generalization causing the many gods to be deposed in favour of one supreme deity regarded as the maker and controller of all things.[1]

This clear cut evolutionary scheme, however, is more in line with the positivistic thought that prevailed in Western Europe in the second half of the nineteenth century under the influence of Comte, Darwin and Tylor than with that of peoples in a primitive state of culture, who have no "thoroughly coherent and rational philosophy". The universal animation of nature and the power exercised over human destinies by beings sharing man's life may be independent of an idea of spiritual doubles or 'separable souls' suggested by reflections, shadows and dream experiences, or of phantoms of the living or the dead. Men of action who live dangerously and precariously have little time or inclination for philosophizing about causes or theorizing about spirits, souls and gods. If, as in the case of a modern child in a civilized community, it is assumed under emotional stress that inanimate objects and events are alive and capable of volitional activity like a human being, this is only because pent-up desires and urgent needs must find an outlet and discharge themselves on tangible objects. Therefore, the primitive assigns conscious will and personal form to things that arouse the sense of awe and reverence, hope and fear. The pre-animistic tendency to 'dance out religion' and express in the rites of the established cult the complex system of sentiments which constitute the essence of orderly social life, calls into being spiritual agencies which assume a will and form appropriate to the occasions and circumstances in which they arise. Upon them man comes to depend more and more for his existence and continuance since by the due observance of the rites of which they are the personification, the seasons are regulated together with such critical events as birth, adolescence, marriage and death. The beneficent and harmful powers of nature have now acquired a conscious

[1] cf. Frazer, *The Worship of Nature*, pages 9f. Tylor, *Primitive Culture*, Vol. I, pages 384ff.

will in the form of a spirit, daimon or god controlling fertility and responsive to human entreaty and ritual control, or when animated by malicious intent, capable of being expelled and rendered innoxious.

But although at this stage in the development of religious reflection the sacred has become personified and localized in perceptible entities associated with particular places, objects and events, and the generalized concept of Providence has assumed a more specific interpretation, it is still operative in and through the prescribed ritual technique. But behind the cultus now lies a hierarchy of spirits, ancestors and gods regarded as efficacious symbols, instruments and agents of divine beneficence or malevolence, endowed with a measure of volitional activity. As localized representations of sacredness and transcendent will, they penetrate and permeate the entire universe, and having acquired attributes and a personality of their own, they exercise particular functions in the control of natural processes and human affairs. Thus, a complex system of animistic and theistic belief and practice has become one of the most conspicuous features in the development of religious thought throughout the ages.

The Cult of Ancestors

How closely interwoven these dogmatic assertions are with the ritual order is seen in the case of the Australian cult of ancestors. In the Alcheringa, or Dream Time of long ago (i.e. the Golden Age), mythical beings are alleged to have lived on the earth and prescribed the laws, customs and cultus to be observed in perpetuity. It was they, as we have seen, who left behind in the wells, creeks and other natural features of the country their life-giving potency, or 'spirit-parts', before retiring from the scene of their creative activity. Henceforth, these sacred spots have become the localized 'totem-centres', or reservoirs of vitality, whence is derived the sacred life of the clan or tribe, and at which the rites of renewal are performed in accordance with the customs and usages prescribed by the ancestors.

There can be little doubt that this ancestral mythology

has arisen out of the topographical ritual organization, and not, as has been often supposed, the ritual from the myth. "Every prominent, and many an insignificant, natural feature" throughout the great central area of the continent, Baldwin Spencer tells us, has some history attached to it,[1] and the Dawn Beings appear to represent the personification of the actions performed at these cult-centres for the purpose of renewing the tribal potency at stated times. At the World Dawn all things were fixed in accordance with the will and purposes of Providence, and as this generalized concept became personified in terms of the Ancestors, the sacred rites were associated with the mythical beings appropriate to the nature of the ceremonies performed at them. In this way the centres were connected with the creative Alchera and their life-giving powers related to the primal source of vitality.

In this cycle of ideas and practices there is nothing to indicate that the ancestors represent either remarkable men raised to divine rank after death, as Herbert Spencer surmised,[2] or, as Tylor imagined, the idea of ghost carried to the highest power.[3] Concern about the pressing problems of everyday life and an intense emotional reaction to the food situation appears to have been the context within which the beliefs have taken shape in close association with their dramatic representation in the traditional ritual. It was, in fact, out of the social and religious organization that the totemic ritual situation arose and this in its turn found expression in the cult of ancestors.

High Gods among Low Races

In addition to these culture heroes, however, there is the shadowy figure of the God of the Mysteries who is thought to have existed before death came into world, and was also responsible for bestowing upon the tribe its laws, customs and beliefs. Among the native tribes of South-eastern

[1] *The Arunta*, page 327.

[2] *Principles of Sociology*, Vol. I, pages 322ff.

[3] *Primitive Culture*, Vol. II, page 334.

Australia, the High Gods, or All-Fathers, are virtually the counterpart of the Alcheringa, or Dawn Ancestors, of the Central and Northern region. In the formative period when all things were in process of creation these Supreme Beings lived on the earth which they themselves had made, and then passed to the seclusion of the sky, or beyond it. Apart from their interest in the initiation rites their chief functions were exercised in the past, and where the Dream Time tradition co-exists with the All-Father beliefs, as among the Kaitish tribe, the High God (called Atnatu) is thought to have made the Alchera. So little, however, has he influenced present conditions that he has ceased to be the God of the Mysteries in this region.

The very remoteness of Supreme Beings tends to reduce them to shadowy forms and sometimes even to bogeys to scare the women and children. Nevertheless, they are a universal feature in primitive society and they cannot be explained as a result of theistic ideas introduced by missionaries or other foreigners. Neither do they represent the idea of ghost or soul carried to the highest power or the deification of chiefs and heroes. Thus, the elaborate researches of Dr. Schmidt, and the evidence produced by the most reliable authorities in all parts of the world, have shown beyond any reasonable measure of doubt that Andrew Lang was correct when, in first calling attention to their existence, he maintained that they constitute an integral part of native belief, independent alike of importation and animistic development. Thus, as Mrs. Langloh Parker revealed,[1] Baiame, the All-Father of the Kamilaroi tribe, was believed to preside over the initiation rites long before Christian ideas had penetrated that part of Australia, while the Kaitish High God, Atnatu, is no glorified ghost of a dead man since he is said to have existed before death came into the world and to have made himself.

While the Supreme Being tends to stand aloof from everyday affairs, he is essentially the personification and guardian of the tribal ethic. Therefore, conduct, determined by the sacredness and inviolability of custom and the established

[1] *Euahlayi Tribe*, pages 5ff.

order, is under his control. In New South Wales, for example, the cardinal sins are dramatically represented and ironically recommended to the novices during the initiation rites over which Daramulun, the All-Father of the Yuin tribe and of those tribes which attend these ceremonies, presides as their instigator. At each stage in the lengthy proceedings moral teaching is given mingled with comic interludes and mimetic dances. The purpose of the rites, in short, is to impress upon those who are being made tribesmen the duties and responsibilities of their office on the authority of the High God whose image is cut in relief on the ceremonial ground. It was he who determined the laws governing the kinship system and instituted the initiation rites for the purpose of inculcating right conduct in society, the rules of which are handed down from generation to generation in these solemn assemblies. Therefore, it is the Supreme Being who is the divine law-giver maintaining tribal conduct in accordance with the principles he established in the beginning.

The Cult of the Bull-roarer

The identification of Daramulun and certain other Australian All-Fathers with the sacred bull-roarer led Dr. Marett to the conclusion that the instrument represents the prototype of High Gods addressed as 'Our Father'. Its thunderous booming he thinks must have been eminently awe-inspiring to the first inventors, or rather discoverers, of the instrument, and would not unnaturally provoke the animistic attributes of life and power to it.[1] Now it is true that Baiame has a duplicate and understudy in Tundum, a name said to mean 'bull-roarer', and that Mungan-ngau among the Jurnai, like Daramulun among the Yuin, speaks with the voice of the bull-roarer. Again, when youths have been initiated in the Arunta tribe they are shown a bull-roarer and it is then explained to them that this is the outward and visible sign of the being named Twanyirika, a secret that on pain of death must never be revealed to the uninitiated. Again, Atnatu, the aforementioned Kaitish All-Father, is said

[1] *The Threshold of Religion*, page 16f.

to have dropped two bull-roarers on the earth which became men who then made wooden bull-roarers to imitate the sound of the god's bull-roarer (i.e. the thunder) in the sky.

The sacredness of this mysterious instrument and its connexion with Supreme Beings, however, are derived from the fact that when it is swung it makes a noise like that of thunder. Therefore, since thunder is almost universally regarded as the voice of a god, and very naturally inspires awe in the minds of those who hear it without understanding how it is actually produced by natural processes, the bull-roarer acquired its sacredness because it reproduces the mysterious sound associated with the divine voice, and therefore with High Gods. Having thus become the sign and symbol of the All-Father, it is revealed to initiates very much as the Holy Sacrament is exposed to the reverent gaze of the faithful in Catholic worship. Inasmuch as no sharp line is drawn in the primitive mind between the sign and the thing signified, the bull-roarer as the thunder-instrument becomes identified with the god whom it represents sacramentally. The unearthly sound with which it is associated produces a numinous experience which Otto would describe in the phrase '*mysterium tremendum*', interpreted in terms of a Power awful and mysterious as the transcendent ground of the visible order. To the primitive mind this appears in the form of a 'magnified non-natural man' speaking with a thunderous voice from the heavens like Yahweh at the holy mount in the Arabian desert.

The Nature and Attributes of Supreme Beings

As the god of the mysteries and personification of the moral order this unique figure stands in sublime majesty as the highest expression of supernatural potency and will, primal and benevolent, the giver and guardian of the good and the right, the supreme originator and upholder of the laws and customs whereby society is maintained as an orderly whole. While in these respects the High Gods of low races resemble the God of the Hebrews, as Andrew Lang and Fr. Schmidt have pointed out, it has to be remembered that it is only within the limits of the primitive mind that the concepts and attributes usually connected with Deity can be applied to tribal All-Fathers. Thus, to say that they existed before death came into the world does not presuppose any conception of time which admits of eternity as a corollary. Similarly, to claim, as do the natives, that they are able "to go anywhere or do anything", does not mean that they are regarded as omnipotent or omniscient except in the sense that such expressions might be applied to a powerful medicine-man. Or again, when they are said to have created the world it is only in the very circumscribed sense bounded by the cosmological outlook of a particular tribe and the creative powers exercised by chiefs and rain-makers, that the words are to be understood.

Moreover, Supreme Beings are by no means always thought to be the controllers of nature like a monotheistic deity. Having made the world, or that part of it with which the group is concerned, the tribal All-Father tends to drop out of the picture except on very special ceremonial occasions, and to pass into obscurity as in the case of the shadowy form of Juok, the High God of the Shilluk people on the White Nile whose worship is eclipsed by that of Nyakang, the popular divine king and deified ancestor of the tribe. Among the Arunta and Luritja in Central Australia, Altjira and Tukura are held to have made nothing and do nothing except eat and hunt and keep harems, while Twanyirika has become a hobgoblin. These otiose Supreme Beings are redundant because they have ceased to exercise a useful and vital function in society and have dissociated themselves from the ritual organization and the social ethic. Therefore, they have degenerated into a mere name or bogey, or a personification of the bull-roarer.

The Absence of Monotheism in Primitive Cult

In every community it would seem there are always a few to whom religion in its loftier and vaguer aspects makes some appeal, but in the case of the majority it is only at certain times—at crises such as birth, marriage, death, harvest and war—that the religious emotion is aroused to any appreciable extent. To the intermittently or indifferently religious High Gods are too high, too disinterested in human affairs, too remote, too hard to live up to, to become popular objects of worship. Therefore, unless the Supreme Being somehow can be brought into direct relation with everyday needs, he is left high and dry in lofty seclusion as "the One Above". When, as in primitive society, the sacred order is too powerful and ever-present to be ignored, the spirits, totems and departmental gods who control natural processes and human destinies, inevitably hold the field because they meet vital requirements in society and exercise all-important functions. This doubtless explains why monotheism has been obscured by polytheism, animism and totemism in primitive cult and the religions of antiquity. And even in modern times such movements as Deism in the eighteenth century were short-lived and ineffective for similar reasons, while the cultus of the saints has never lacked its votaries.

Genuine monotheism is unknown in primitive society because the tribal All-Father fails to meet the entire needs of the community, and though, as has been indicated above, he may be in some way related to the ritual organization on special occasions, Dr. Radin may be correct in thinking that he was not meant to be worshipped.[1] Be this as it may, in practice Supreme Beings have seldom been approached in prayer and sacrifice in the same way and to the same extent as lesser divinities, and since supernatural power is exercised through a ritual technique, to be effective gods must be ritually accessible, efficacious and controllable.

Culture-heroes and the Kingship

Take for example the divine ancestor and culture-hero Nyakang, the traditional founder and first king of the Shilluk. He is said to have led the people to the land they occupy, to have made them great, given them their laws, regulated

[1] *Primitive Religion* (London, 1938), page 266.

their marriage customs, divided the country into districts and bestowed rain upon it. Then he disappeared mysteriously in a storm like the wind, but he has ever since continued to manifest himself from time to time in certain animals, or alight on a tree as a bird, as well as to live on from age to age in the reigning monarch in whom his spirit is immanent. Prayers and sacrifices are offered to him and at ten shrines he is venerated. Before the annual rains begin a bullock is killed at the door of one of the sacred huts while the king calls upon his divine ancestor to intercede with Juok, the High God, to renew the face of the earth with life-giving showers. When the millet has been gathered a portion of the grain is taken to the shrines, ground into flour and made into porridge. Some of the porridge is poured out on the threshold of the hut, some of it is smeared on the outer walls and the rest is emptied on the ground outside. Therefore, while the Supreme Being (Juok) is the ultimate source of beneficence, it is the ancestor Nyakang, and his human representative the king, who are the actual intermediaries in the renewal of life and of divine bounty.

Thus, it is to the anthropomorphic figure of the man-god that men turn for succour as the living reality who, having lived on the earth in human form and caused life and order to spring forth from death and chaos, is ever-present in the person of his royal embodiment and accessible in the established cultus. But it is not enough to have originated laws and culture. The culture-hero, or transformer as he is sometimes called, must live on and continue to influence the world and human destinies if he too is not to pass into a limbo of obscurity as a shadowy figure like the High God. The Egyptian saviour-god Osiris may have been an ancient king who taught men agriculture and irrigation, as has been suggested, but he acquired survival value because he secured permanence in the cultus through the immortal figure of his son Horus, the prototype of the living king. Thus, Osiris and Horus came to personify the recurrent cycle of life through death in nature and in mankind.

Functioning as the high priest *par excellence*, the Pharaoh in Ancient Egypt daily performed his ritual tasks as the representative both of the Sun-god in the sky and culture-hero on earth, when the solar theology was brought into relation with that of Osiris. Thus he combined in his complex personality the character and attributes of a High God and a fertility deity, being at once a creator and sustainer of the right order of nature, author and giver of life and the dynamic cohesive centre of society. This dual aspect of the kingship is a characteristic feature of the religious and social organization of the urban civilization of the Ancient East. It recurs in Mesopotamia where the king was regarded as the earthly descendant of the great gods, Anu, Enlil, Sin and Marduk, who were also givers of fertility. In Syria it occupies a prominent place in the recently discovered ritual texts at Ras Shamra as part of the liturgical drama, while it is fundamental in the mystery cults throughout the Eastern Mediterranean. Therefore, it is not improbable that it represents an early attempt to bring the remote sky-god into a definite relationship with life on earth.

The High God and the Fertility God

As in all polytheistic systems, culture contact doubtless played its part in fusing into a composite mythology and ritual organization gods who originally had very different attributes and histories. Nevertheless, as we have seen, life-giving powers are characteristic qualities of Supreme Beings in their creative aspects before they become otiose. Sometimes it is true, as in the case of Baiame, the control of nature is delegated to another deity, such as the Rainbow-Serpent in Australia, but since invariably their dwelling is in the heavens, once they become associated with the sun the way is opened for them to exercise a powerful influence over the growth of vegetation in agricultural society. The sun and rain being the essential requirements of fecundity in nature, the god who controls these two vital elements can hardly fail to acquire a fertility significance. The old Egyptian Sun-god, in fact, was called "he who originates from himself," and throughout the history of religion light and life have always been synonymous.

Therefore, when the cult of the Sun-god became the care of the king, begotten of his heavenly father, the life of the sky was as it were brought to earth and made accessible by the due performance of the prescribed royal solar ritual. In short, the Supreme God, rescued from oblivion, was now able to exercise his life-giving functions on earth as, or in conjunction with, a fertility deity. But in so doing he had to abandon any pretence of monotheistic exclusiveness. While unquestionably he enjoyed the prestige and predominance of his heavenly estate, he was, nevertheless, only one among many divinities who played their several rôles in the economy of a developing civilization. At most, like the Greek Zeus on Mount Olympus, who apparently also began his career in the sky, the Sun-god was "a great king above all gods" rejoicing as a strong man to run his course with his subordinates. Even in his or her own domain, the moon has always been a powerful rival, featuring often as a mother goddess and therefore intimately concerned with the processes of fertility, and not infrequently with the cult of the dead. The stars as the offspring of the sun and moon, tend to occupy a subordinate position in the celestial hierarchy, and sometimes they are regarded as human souls translated to the sky after death as semi-divine beings.

The Development of Polytheism

As in the heavens so on earth a plurality of personalities characterize polytheistic communities, each divinity having a name and sphere of activity of its own so that in the welter of gods the unity of divine power and will is resolved into a sacred world of many potencies. From time to time, however, attempts have been made to fuse into the single form of a particular deity the qualities and attributes of an entire pantheon. Thus, in Mesopotamia, the tendency to group and grade gods in hierarchies as the patrons of cities and controllers of the various aspects of nature, led to the exaltation of one god as the head of the pantheon, and the absorption by him of the prerogatives of the rest. At Nippur, for instance, one of the oldest centres in the Euphrates valley,

Enlil, the chief of the storm gods, not only presided over the city but ruled over the earth, while the goddess Ishtar, who was especially worshipped at Aruk, was the patroness of fertility. When in due course the solar god of Babylon, Marduk, succeeded to the primacy, he acquired the attributes of Enlil and took his consort, Ninlil, to be his wife in true anthropomorphic fashion, like his prototype Tammuz who consorted with Ishtar as the dying and reviving vegetation deity.

Combining in his person the features of a sun-god with those of a fertility-god, Marduk became the controller of the seasons as well as "the lord of the lands" over which he ruled by virtue of his primordial victory over the winged monster, Tiamat, the arch enemy of the gods. Having ordered the universe anew and made a covering for the heavens with half of her severed body, he set the stations for the great gods in the likeness of constellations. The moon became the ruler of the night, but as "king of the heavens" he identified himself with Jupiter, the largest of the planets and, as it was supposed, ruler of the stars. Thus, as one of the creation tablets has it, "he pastured the gods like sheep," and in order that their service might be established on the earth he had created from the body of Tiamat, he proceeded to fashion man out of the blood of her lover, Kingu; or, as another version of the story says, with his own blood and that of the gods. He then received the titles of all the other gods, identifying himself with them collectively. Nergal is called "the Marduk of war," Nebo "the Marduk of property," Enlil "the Marduk of sovereignty," Ninib "the Marduk of strength," and so on. But although he absorbed the rest of the pantheon, the other gods did not cease to have an independent existence and to exercise their proper functions, while Ishtar remained as powerful a personality as her male counterpart, Tammuz, whose rôle Marduk had inherited.

The Beginnings of Monotheism

In Egypt an effort was made in the Eighteenth Dynasty (*c.* 1375 B.C.) by Amenhotep IV, or Ikhnaton as he called himself, to break away from the polytheistic tradition altogether, and transform the Sun-god into a genuinely monotheistic deity. Hitherto, under the name of Amon-Re, the Sun had been regarded as a composite god like Marduk, and sometimes he had been described as Aton, an ancient designation of the physical sun associated particularly with the disk from which it appears to shine on the world. But the Theban members of the New Kingdom had equated their own deity, Amon, the god of Thebes, with Re, the ancient Sun-god, as the Supreme God of Egypt, who exercised his jurisdiction over the many lands which at that time constituted the empire, extending from the Euphrates to the islands of the Aegean and the fourth cataract of the Nile. Thus, Amon-Re assumed a universal character as an imperial deity—"the sole lord taking captive all lands every day," and as Atum, "the Creator of mankind, who distinguished their nature and made their life". Therefore, in his dual capacity Amon-Re moved in the direction of monotheism, summing up in his nature and attributes the principal qualities of the God of all the earth.

Amenhotep IV, however, was a devotee of Aton, whom he regarded as "the sole God whose powers no other possesseth". It was he who "created the earth according to his heart while he was alone ; set every man in his place and supplieth their necessities," and made "the Nile in the Nether World and the Nile in the sky". For the remaining eleven years of his life after his accession to the throne, the young king and his wife, the beautiful Nefertiti, devoted themselves to the propagation of the new monotheistic movement centred in the worship of the symbol of the solar disk. The simplicity and beauty of this faith is revealed in the "Hymn to the Sun" in which the universal splendour and power of Aton is extolled in language hardly surpassed in any of the higher religions, and strongly reminiscent of the 104th Psalm in Hebrew literature, as may be seen from the following quotations :

> When thou goest down in the western horizon,
> The earth is in darkness as if it were dead. . . .
> Every lion cometh forth from his den,

And all snakes that bite. . . .
When it is dawn and thou risest in the horizon and shinest as
  the sun in the day,
Thou dispellest the darkness and sheddest thy beams.
The two lands keep festival, awake, and stand on their feet,
For thou hast raised them up.
They wash their bodies,
They take their clothes,
Their hands (are lifted) in adoration to thy rising.
The whole land doeth its work. (Cf. Ps. civ. 20-23.)

Or again,

How manifold are thy works,
They are hidden from me,
O sole God, to whom none is to be likened. . . .
The earth is in thy hand,
For thou hast made them.
When thou arisest they live,
When thou settest they die.
Thou art life in thyself,
Men live through thee.
The eyes look on thy beauty,
Until thou settest. (Cf. Ps. civ. 24, 27-30.)

The earlier Cairo Hymn to Amon (1447-1420 B.C.), however, is on much the same level and from it doubtless Ikhnaton derived his inspiration. Nevertheless, he gave expression to a conception of monotheism which is genuinely unique as an organized movement not only in Egypt but in the history of religion. It was too short-lived, however, to make any permanent impression on the faith of the country or of the world. At his death the nation, rallied by the dispossessed Amonite priesthood, speedily returned to its former gods, and every effort was made to efface the work of the heretical king. Thus faded into oblivion the first vision of the sole rule of one God, centred in and symbolized by the all-enveloping sun.

Whether or not this impressive movement owed anything to Semitic influence is difficult to say. Ikhnaton, it is true, was the son of Tii, a proto-Nordic princess of the race of Mitanni, and his queen came from the same region north of the Euphrates, a district associated with the name of the Hebrew patriarch Abraham. But the monotheism of the Old Testament differs fundamentally from that of the Ikhnaton movement, or, indeed, of any corresponding monotheistic tendencies in the Ancient East. The Hebrews, who were never addicted to solar worship, originally practised an animistic and polytheistic cultus not very different from that of the rest of the nomadic desert stock to which they belonged (generalized under the name Aramaean), except that they rescued from oblivion a widely dispersed West Semitic High God, sometimes known as *El*, at other times as *Ya*, *Yau* or *Yawe*. Under the influence of their leader Moses he was made the jealous god of the tribes when they were consolidated into a nation unified by a convenant relationship with him as his 'peculiar people'. It was not denied, of course, that other countries had their gods who were legitimately worshipped within their own borders, but, so far as Israel was concerned, Yahweh alone was the object of worship and allegiance. This remained the contention of the 'monotheistic' minority (if the worshippers of an exclusive *national* god can be so described) throughout the checkered history of the Hebrews. The people as a whole were always inclined to patronize the local vegetation gods, or baalim, of Palestine, but the mono-Yahwists, deriving their inspiration from the theophany to Moses in the desert, never wavered in their strenuous efforts to eradicate in Israel the Canaanite cultus. But it was not until after the Exile in Babylon in the sixth century B.C. that genuine monotheism was established in Judaism, although unquestionably the work of Moses and his successors made the shadowy figure of the All-Father of the nomadic tribes the central fact in the religious and social life of the nation.

In origin, Yahweh was essentially an anthropomorphic Supreme Being rather than a solar or nature deity like Marduk, Amon-Re or Aton. Moreover, his main concern was with the people whom he had adopted and to whom it was maintained he had revealed himself at the Holy Mount and the burning bush, ratifying his covenant with them from time to time through supernatural interventions on their behalf. So far from being remote and disinterested in human affairs, he was the centre of the cultus which became the rallying point and unifying principle in the community, first in the form of the Ark of the Covenant and later in the temple worship on Mount Zion. Under the influence of the prophetic movement in the eighth century B.C., he acquired an ethical significance, and after the Exile he was given universal sovereignty as the omnipotent Lord of all the earth in comparison with whom all the gods of the surrounding nations were but idols. "I am the Lord and there is none else, beside me there is no god" (Is. xlv, 5f.). It was he who created the heavens and formed the earth, visiting it and watering it, causing the grass to grow for the cattle and the herb for the oxen, establishing the moon and the sun, and ordering summer and winter (Gen. i, 1, Ps. lxv, 9-13, lxxiv, 16f.). Thus, while he retained the characteristic qualities of a Supreme Being in primitive society, and in pre-exilic Israel consorts were assigned to him under such names as Anath-Bethel, Anath-Yahu, Ashim-Bethel, in him was preserved unity of will and consistency of purpose in the government of the world and of men in greater measure than in the other monotheistic traditions in the religions of antiquity. Furthermore, as the consolidating centre of a theocrasy, he gave solidarity and continuity to the social structure which enabled a remnant of the nation to survive such a disintegrating catastrophe as that of the Exile, and to re-establish its life and worship around its ancient ritual organization. The achievement of Israel lay in rescuing Yahweh from oblivion as a remote High God by making *history* the scene of his activity and the supreme revelation of his purpose and power.

BIBLIOGRAPHY

Breasted, J. H. *Religion and Thought in Ancient Egypt.* London, 1912.

Cook, S. A. *The Old Testament : a Reinterpretation.* London, 1936.

Hocart, A. M. *Kings and Councillors.* Cairo, 1936.

Hooke, S. H. *Myth and Ritual.* Oxford, 1933.
Howitt, A. W. *Native Tribes of South-east Australia.* London, 1904.
Lang, A. *The Making of Religion.* London, 1898.
Lods, A. *Israel.* E. T. by S. H. Hooke. London, 1932.
Radin, P. *Monotheism among Primitive Peoples.* London, 1924.
Primitive Religion. London, 1938.
Schmidt, W. *The Origin and Growth of Religion.* London, 1931.
Seligman, C. G. *Cult of the Nyakang and the Divine Kings of the Shilluk.* Khartoum, 1911.
Söderblom, N. *The Living God.* Oxford, 1931.
Tylor, E. B. *Primitive Culture.* London, 1871.
Westermann, D. *The Shilluk People, their Language and Folk Lore.* Berlin, 1912.

CHAPTER IV

SACRIFICE AND SACRAMENT

THE foregoing analysis of primitive ritual and belief has revealed that religion performs its proper function in society through an organized cultus. Of the many rites that have been employed for this purpose the institution of sacrifice has gained a position of pre-eminence in most of the higher religions and we have now to investigate the earlier and more rudimentary phases of this type of ritual.

The Institution of Sacrifice

From time immemorial, as Tylor and others have pointed out, offerings have been made to supernatural beings to secure their favour or to minimize their hostility, but while the making a gift to a deity as if he were a man doubtless has played its part in the development of sacrifice, many other ideas and motives have entered into this composite ritual. Thus, for example, Robertson Smith in his lectures on *The Religion of the Semites*, called attention to the importance of the communal meal as a means of establishing a bond of union between the god identified within the sacred food and those who consume it. And sacrifice (from the Latin *sacrificium ; sacer* 'holy' and *facere* 'to make') is essentially a rite in the course of which something is forfeited or destroyed in order to establish a right and beneficial relationship with a transcendent source of strength and vitality. The destruction of the victim is incidental and accessory, however, to the liberation of the life and power inherent in the object sacrificed, since it is the inherent potency that is imparted to the god or his worshippers for a variety of purposes which we have now to examine.

In the first instance sacrifice is part of the process of giving life to promote or preserve life which, we have seen, is a principle very deeply laid in the history of religion. This is most apparent in the case of the blood offering. As the vital essence blood is the animating principle, or soul-substance, the mysterious power of which has been believed to be potent whether within the body or without. Hence the widespread taboos surrounding this supernaturally dangerous sacred substance and the numerous ritual uses to which it has been put. The Jews were strictly forbidden to partake of it "for as to the life of all flesh, the blood thereof is all one with the life thereof ; whosoever eateth it shall be cut off" (Lev. xvii, 10f.). Being consecrated wholly to Yahweh men were prohibited from consuming it, their share of the offerings being the flesh (I. Sam. xiv, 34f., Exod. xxix, 16, Lev. i, 5, viii, 15, ix, 9). But though the special 'life' associated with the blood was strictly reserved for the god of Israel, his worshippers were given some share in the vitalizing properties of the victim since they were also present in certain internal organs, such as the liver, the intestines, the caul, the kidneys and the fat upon them (Exod. xxix, 3), though even these were sometimes taboo (Lev. iii, 17, I Sam. ii, 16). But the blood might still be sprinkled on them to cement their union with their god, as it is also said to have been applied to their door-posts at the time of the Exodus to prevent 'the destroyer' entering their dwellings (Exod. xii, 7, 23).

These taboos suggest, however, as Robertson Smith pointed out, that formerly a communal meal was held on the flesh and blood of the victim as the life-giving agent to man as well as to the deity, before the blood was wholly set apart for Yahweh, very much as in totemic society the sacred species is solemnly eaten once a year to imbibe its sacrosanct life and to consolidate the members of the food group in a sacramental alliance. In these acts of communion the totem is not a sacrificial victim, at once god and kinsman, as Robertson Smith supposed. It is the potent agent in consolidating the tribe in a blood brotherhood in a common alliance with the sacred order.

The Blood Covenant

This is symbolized by the blood bond as participation in a common vital essence concentrated in a higher unity in the sacred ally. Thus, the group is united in a totemic relationship so that the members become 'all-one-flesh' in a sacramental sense, and this union is strengthened and renewed through a common meal on sacred food in which the tribal soul-substance is present with all its potency as a consolidating and regenerative agent, binding the individuals together more firmly in a blood brotherhood. But the communion sought is with the totem rather than with the food itself, and through the totem with the members of the totemic group in society. Thus, at this rudimentary stage in the development of the sacramental principle, man is reaching out towards the inward and spiritual through the outward and visible in an attempt to establish a religious bond, or *sacramentum*, with the transcendent species in a mystery in which the group and its ally lose their separate identities in a common ancestry and animating essence.

The Sacramental Principle

In Roman law the word *sacramentum* was used to describe a legal religious sanction in which a man placed his life or property in the hands of the supernatural powers who upheld justice. It then became an oath of obedience taken by soldiers to their *imperator*, sworn under a formula having a religious significance. But since both the Latin *sacer* and the Greek *mysterion* signify that which is set apart or taboo because it belongs to the sacred order, the word *sacramentum* has become a convenient term to describe efficacious signs or symbols which convey something 'hidden'—a mysterious potency transmitted through a ritual act. In this sense it was adopted by the Church in the third century for its appointed ordinances, whereby divine grace was imparted to the soul of man. Eventually, in the twelfth century, it was narrowed down in Western Christendom to seven specific rites, though, in a looser sense, any ceremony endowing a person or thing with a sacred character (e.g., blessing holy water or incense, churching women, or giving alms for a particular purpose) had a sacramental significance.

All the deepest emotions, experiences and evaluations of human beings in every state of culture find expression by means of actions and objects which are made the vehicle of their actualization in time and space, so that 'inward' and 'outward' experience meets in a higher unity which guarantees the latter its full validity. Thus, mental and spiritual activity is only known as embodied, the embodiment being not a symbol but an 'effectual sign' of a mental or spiritual act. Thought cannot exist without a localized centre, or thinking object, which mediates and conditions the initial responses, and presents objects, sounds, smells, and other components of its experience and consciousness to the senses or the imagination. Therefore, at all times and on every cultural horizon the human mind functions symbolically, but, as Dr. Edwyn Bevan has pointed out, there are two different kinds of symbols. There are visible objects or sounds which stand for something of which we already have direct knowledge, such as, for instance, the Union Jack or the Cenotaph. These are more than a multi-coloured piece of cloth or a block of stone; but while they are the emblems of the nation, they do not give a patriotic Briton any information about his country, or the part it has played in the world of things which he knows otherwise. There are, however, other kinds of symbols which purport to give information about the nature of the things they symbolize not otherwise known, and beyond the range of human experience.[1]

In the domain of religion it is to this latter class that the sacramental principle belongs. "No man hath seen God at any time," and the spiritual world can only be visualized and made actual under temporal conditions by means of symbols or signs. Certain 'rare souls' with unusual mystic gifts or occult powers appear to be able to reach a perception of the timeless, spaceless presence of the transcendental without these material aids. Nevertheless, even the oriental mystics not infrequently resort to such devices as yoga in the contemplation of the Infinite, while in Western Christendom contemplatives invariably have had regular recourse to the prescribed sacramental institutions of the Church. But since human beings are accustomed to think symbolically and make pictures out of the materials presented by the senses, normally ultimate reality and the mysterious presence of the *numen*, are perceived phenomenally by means of effectual signs through the instrumentality of matter.

In primitive society everyday events have been given a sacramental significance by investing them with a supernatural meaning in relation to the ultimate source of all beneficence. Temporal needs are made to depend on a proper relation being maintained with the unseen powers, and the health and well-being of society demand the recognition of a hierarchy of values of which the lower is always dependent upon the higher, and the highest is self-sufficient. This transcendent source of values outside and above human life, essential to the stability of the whole scheme, becomes operative in a sacramental system in which the material is instrumental to the actualization of the spiritual and guarantees the validity of the outward experience, so that the purposive order holds its own against the merely casual. To partake of the flesh of a sacrificial victim, or of a cereal image of a vegetation deity, makes the eater a recipient of divine life and qualities, just as in funerary ritual portions of the dead are consumed to imbibe their attributes, or sometimes to ensure their reincarnation. Conversely, the mourners

[1] *Symbolism and Belief* (London, 1938), page 11f.

allow their blood to fall on the corpse in order to give new life to the deceased and to renew the blood covenant with a departed kinsman.

The Origins of Sacrifice

In this cycle of sacramental and sacrificial ideas and practices it is the giving of life that is really fundamental. The eating of sacred food and the ritual shedding of blood are the means whereby life is given to promote and preserve life and to establish a bond of union with the supernatural order. In food gathering communities these observances are directed mainly on the control of the chase and the propagation of the species. But with the introduction of agriculture and the domestication of animals, they are concentrated upon the king as the dynamic centre of fertility. Where this office has not been exercised by divine kings, as for example, in Ancient Rome, the *sacrificium* was part of the household cult and consisted of simple offerings at the daily family meal at which, as Ovid reminds us, the gods were thought to be present.[1] Portions of the food were thrown into the fire for the household gods to make them favourable just as similar bloodless oblations were made of the cereals in the fields. It was only on exceptional occasions that the blood offering featured in the worship of the early Latin farmers, and then it was confined to pigs, sheep and the cow or the ox, representing the three chief animal products of the farm, with goats at the feast known as the Lupercalia, and a dog at that called the Robigalia. Prior to the emergence of the State-cult, a priesthood and temple worship were unknown in this region, in marked distinction from the elaborate sacrificial cultus of the great urban civilizations in the Ancient East, where originally the institution grew up and took shape round the slaying of the man-god as the incarnation of the vegetation principle and the embodiment of the gods on whom it depended.

As the instrument of Providence controlling divine beneficence, the king became at once the victim and the chief worshipper. For reasons which have been explained,[2]

[1] *Fasti*, vi, 305 ; 6.

[2] cf., pages 62ff.

the custom arose at an early period of putting the reigning chief or monarch to death after a fixed number of years, or when his natural vigour showed signs of waning, or when the crops failed. This practice, common until recently in Africa and the islands of the Pacific, was often modified or relaxed altogether by the provision of a substitute for the royal victim. Thus, we have seen that in Mexico the Aztecs had a mock-king in the person of a young and vigorous prisoner of war who, after fulfilling his tragic office for a year, paid the supreme penalty in lieu of the real monarch whom he impersonated. But human sacrifice, whether of kings or commoners, has never been a permanent institution and sooner or later, substitutes have been provided either in the form of animal victims or in that of ritual devices, such as those employed in the renewal ceremonies at the Sed-festival in Egypt, or at the temporary abdication of the king during the New Year rites in the temple of Marduk in Babylon.

The Offering of the Firstborn

Nevertheless, the divine king was the proper person to immolate himself on behalf of his people when his vitality declined, and failing him, if the principle of substitution were admitted, a prince of the royal blood—for preference the eldest son of the reigning monarch—should take his place on the altar. It is this custom, doubtless, that lies behind the Greek legend of the misadventures of the unfortunate Athamas, whose eldest male descendants were always liable to be sacrificed to save the crops.[1] The peculiar sanctity attached to the firstborn of man and beast, render them liable to this fate since in primitive society the liberation of their life has always been thought to be especially efficacious in renewal ritual. Thus, on the assumption that an offering of such potency would have a re-invigorating effect on all actual and potential members of the household, the tribes on the North-western coast of America frequently sacrificed the first male child to ensure

[1] *Herodotus*, vii, 197.

the health and vigour of the rest of the family. In Uganda the firstborn of the chief if a male was strangled by the midwife to prevent the death of his father through the transference of his vitality to his eldest son. Even so, notwithstanding this drastic precaution, an orgy of human sacrifice was still required at his coronation, and at stated periods during his reign, to maintain his physical strength, the principal victim being the son of a chief who was treated as a prince.

In the familiar story of the proposed offering of Isaac by Abraham recorded in the Book of Genesis (xxii, 1-14), and in the immolation in the Greek legend of Iphigenia, a relic of this custom seems to have survived; though the Jews and Greeks sought to supply animal substitutes for human beings. It can hardly be doubted, however, that in the beginning the god of Israel was thought to demand the firstborn of man and beast, as the most ancient document in the Book of Exodus suggests (Exod. xxii, 29f (E), cf. Exod. iii, 2 (P)), before it was commuted into a payment of money by way of redemption (Exod. xiii, 12f., xxiv, 20), or, as in the later Priestly version, where the Levites are taken instead of the firstlings (Num. iii, 11ff.- 40ff.). But so deeply laid is the practice in Hebrew tradition, that as Frazer has pointed out, the one thing that looms clear through the haze of the Paschal festival is "the memory of a great massacre of firstborn" which occurred apparently at the critical vernal equinox when the moon was full.[1] All the circumstances of this observance suggest that it was originally a vegetation rite, though whether the victim taken from the flocks and herds was a substitute for an offering of the firstborn children of the year, is not easy to determine. It is not improbable that at first the oblation was made on behalf of the king to secure the prosperity of the land in the spring, as elsewhere, but if this were so, a lamb or a kid without blemish had long replaced the human offering. Since to have carried out the injunction, literally, would have involved too great a drain on the resources of the population, some modification of the law was inevitable.

[1] *The Golden Bough*, Part IV, pages 176ff.

That child sacrifice was fairly common in Palestine before the Israelite occupation is suggested by the numerous skeletons of children in jars and urns found at Gezer, Taanach, Tell-el-Hesy and Megiddo in the foundations of temples, houses, fortresses and city-walls, together with the bodies of some adults, to give strength to the buildings. Moreover, Hiel the Bethelite is said to have laid the foundations of the restored walls of Jericho "in his firstborn", and set up the gates "in his youngest son" (Josh. vi, 26, I Kings xvi, 34). If the precise meaning of this statement is open to doubt, the story of the fulfilment of his vow on the part of Jephthah (Jud. lxi, 30ff.), and the passing of children through the fire to Moloch (i.e. the king) in the valley of Hinnom (II Kings xxiii, 10), show that human sacrifice was taken for granted in pre-exilic Israel despite all efforts to eliminate it. It is not improbable, in fact, that it was one of the contributory causes of the opposition of the Hebrew prophets to an institution which they regarded as inseparable from all the abuses of vegetation ritual (Amos v, 25, Hos. vi, 6, Jer. vii, 22f.).

The Offering of the First-fruits

That animals should frequently take the place of human beings as sacrificial victims follows naturally from the mystic bond that in primitive society is thought to exist between man and certain sacred species. This relationship is exemplified in the cult of guardian spirits and in totemism, and, judging from the representations of masked dancers figured in the Palaeolithic caves, the affinity is very deeply laid in the history of religion. Consequently, if there is no essential distinction between the two forms of life, human and animal, there is no adequate reason why the one should not replace the other on the altar. But it is not only animals that have been regarded as the blood brothers of man and the reservoir for the potency of the tribe. Any object manifesting growth and fecundity is similarly interpreted as a symbol of vitality and assigned fertilizing properties. Thus, the Ainu not only offer a bear-cub at their Annual Festival but treat in an identical manner cakes made of the first-fruits of the millet. These they address as "the cereal divinity" and beseech it to nourish them before they eat it sacramentally. The Thompson Indians of British Columbia, before consuming the new berries, roots and other products of the season, make a similar prayer to a being called "the sunflower-root" whom they allege they are about to eat as "the greatest of all in mystery".

Among the Aztecs in Mexico, during the May Festival in honour of Uitzilopochtli, a huge statue of the god was fashioned by virgins in dough in which a quantity of beet seed and roasted maize were mingled and moulded with honey. It was then covered with a rich garment by noblemen and placed in a chair on a litter to be carried in procession to the foot of a great pyramid-shaped temple, accompanied by maidens in white and young men in red robes, both crowned with garlands of maize. In the court below the flight of steps up which they conveyed the idol to a shrine filled with roses, the people stood in reverence and awe, and the virgins brought innumerable pieces of paste compounded of beets and roasted maize made in the shape of large bones, which the young men laid at the feet of the idol. From the other temples priests and attendants adorned with garlands of flowers and veils of diverse colours, each according to his rank, joined the throng of worshippers, and were followed by images of their gods and goddesses similarly attired. Assembling themselves around the dough figure, the consecration rites began, the purpose of which was to transform the pieces of paste into the flesh and bones of the cereal deity. A number of victims were then sacrificed and a strict fast was observed in preparation for the solemn eating of the consecrated paste figure, which was broken into small fragments. After all had partaken of this sacred food, including the women and children, the sick were communicated in their houses.[1]

In December, at the winter solstice, the god was killed

[1] J. de Acosta, *Natural and Moral History of the Indies* (Hakluyt Society, London, 1880), Book V, chapter xxiv, Vol. II, pages 356ff.

in effigy, the dough of which the image was composed having been fortified with the blood of children. The bones of the deity were represented by pieces of acacia wood, and the image thus constructed was placed on the principal altar in the temple to be censed by the king. The following day it was stood on its feet in a great hall to be 'slain' by a priest impersonating Quetzalcoatl, the Toltec culture hero, who pierced it with a flint dart. The heart of the image was cut out by a priest and given to the king to eat, while the rest of it was broken up into small pieces to be solemnly consumed by all the male members of the community. But women were forbidden to receive at this festival, known as the "killing of the god Uitzilopochtli". Similar images of dough were eaten sacramentally at other feasts in Mexico after their heads had been cut off and hearts torn out.[1]

The purpose of these sacrificial communions was that of securing good health and a renewal of strength. The food was charged with the potency and supernatural qualities of the deity represented by its duly consecrated image and surrogate. In North America the Natchez of Louisana held a "feast of grain" in the seventh moon when the chief known as the Great Sun was seated in his royal capacity on a litter upon the shoulders of warriors like the Aztec cereal image, and carried to a round granary outside the village. There he alighted, having first saluted the new corn thrice, and sat on his throne. New fire was made by friction and when everything was prepared for dressing the corn, it was solemnly cooked and distributed to the female Suns, and then to all the women, who carried it with haste to their huts to prepare it. This accomplished, the Great Sun presented a plate of it to the four quarters of the earth, and ordered first the warriors and then the boys and women to eat it in their huts. Throughout the night a torchlight dance was held, and the following day two troops, led by the Great Sun and the Chief of War respectively, engaged in a violent contest with a ball of deer-skin. The proceedings concluded with the

[1] Sahagun, *Histoire générale des choses de la Nouvelle Espagne*, pages 203ff . . . 33.

Great Sun being carried back on his litter, and the return of the people to their village.[1]

The great sanctity with which the new crops were regarded in the Mississippi valley and the wilderness to the east of the river, is shown by the drastic preparations for the observance in the Creek country in July and August, when the corn was ripe. In addition to the extinguishing of all the fires in the village, the scouring of the cooking vessels, the sweeping of the public square by warriors, a strict fast was observed for two nights and a day which involved purgings with emetics. New fire was then kindled by the high priest and placed on the altar in the temple, and a basket of new fruits was offered "to the bountiful holy spirit of fire, as a first-fruit offering and an animal oblation for sin". The purifications completed, the new crops were dressed on the new fires and eaten with bear's oil, the men rubbing the corn between their hands and on their faces and breasts. For eight days the ceremonies continued and towards the end of the festival the warriors fought a mock battle. Continence was strictly observed throughout, and not till the end did the men and women dance together ; a survival perhaps of a sacred marriage. Finally, having smeared themselves with white clay, they bathed in running water to complete their purification and regeneration.[2]

Since the permission of the chief was sought before the new crops were eaten, it is not improbable that the act of desacralization was a precaution against their being gathered too soon, but, nevertheless, it was their inherent sacredness that rendered them taboo and gave them their sacramental character. Sometimes, as among the Ainu and the Thompson Indians, the mysterious vitality was interpreted in terms of a 'cereal deity' or 'corn spirit'. In other cases it was more in the nature of an impersonal soul-substance capable of transference through a ritual meal, and, like the Polynesian

[1] J. R. Swanton, 43*rd Bulletin Bureau Amer; Ethnol.* (Washington, 1911), pages 115ff.

[2] F. G. Speck, *Ethnology of the Yuki Indians* (Philadelphia, 1909), pages 86f. C. MacCauley, 5*th R.B.A.E.* (Washington, 1887), pages 522ff, for the Seminole rites.

kava, the Vedic Soma, the Avestan haoma and the Greek ambrosia, it was endowed with supernatural properties as a life-giving agent. Thus, the drinking of these sacred beverages, which originally seems to have been confined to chiefs and kings in their divine capacity, bestowed health, wisdom and immortality by virtue of the qualities imparted to them at their consecration.

Similarly, the effigies composed of newly cut seedlings, or the last sheaf of corn in which the vegetation spirit is thought to reside in the form of a maiden or an old woman, impart the supernatural powers and properties inherent in the first-fruits. When the corn-spirit is regarded as a 'mother', as in Styria, the image is made by one of the elder women of the village, and the finest ears are plucked out of it to form a wreath which is carried by the prettiest girl. The effigy is placed on the top of a pile of wood during the harvest supper and dance, and then it is hung up in the barn till the threshing is over and the wreath is dedicated in church. At Christmas the image is placed in the crib to make the cattle thrive, and on Holy Saturday a seventeen year old girl rubs the grain out of it and scatters it among the young corn.

Behind rites of this nature, which are of universal occurrence in the peasant cultures of Central Europe and elsewhere, is the idea of ensuring the continuance of the crops through the transmission of the potency inherent in either the first-fruits or the last sheaf, symbolized by the figure of the Great Mother as the source of fertility. But the cutting and ingathering of the crops involves what is virtually the sacrifice of the indwelling vegetation spirit so that harvest becomes intimately associated with the ancient theme of the dying and reviving god. Consequently, there is also present in this ritual the fear of incurring the revenge of the slain divinity, resulting in either the failure of the crops (i.e. withdrawing her fertilizing powers), or vengeance descending upon those responsible for her death. Thus, in the Highlands of Scotland there was a struggle to escape from being the last to cut the corn lest "the famine of the farm", in the shape of an old woman called the Cailleach, should have to be fed until the following harvest. Moreover, the possession of this dreaded legacy was calculated to bring disaster upon the unfortunate last reaper on whom she descended. The vegetation spirit, therefore, is associated with death as well as with life and becomes virtually a sacrificial victim.

Expiation and Atonement

Since the slaying of the Corn-mother involves also the removal of the evil impeding the stream of life, the negative side of the institution of sacrifice falls within this framework of ideas and practices. Demonic power residing in the soil and its products, it has to be rendered harmless by an expulsion and expiatory ritual regarded as an atoning sacrifice. Death has to be met by a fresh outpouring of life on behalf of the person making the oblation thereby re-establishing a right and beneficial relationship with the sacred order, or the god who personifies Providence.

To the primitive mind the good being primarily life, health and prosperity, and evil famine, barrenness and death, each under the control of transcendent forces, to secure providential beneficence that which hinders and impedes it must be removed by appropriate ritual methods. Any unusual misfortune or disaster is a manifestation of divine displeasure and demands a concrete act of propitiation by way of atonement to remove the cause and occasion of the evil. Since the anger of the gods finds expression in the failure of the crops, outbreaks of plague and disease and similar calamities, attributed to some ritual error or defilement, reconciliation is effected by means of purifying agents, such as water and blood, or a 'scapegoat' (i.e. an animal or human being employed as a 'sin-remover'). This generally involves the death of a victim, or the destruction of an object, to liberate its life-giving qualities as a sacrificial oblation to appease the wrath of the god and remove the pollution. In this case a life is offered to save life, and expiation is the 'wiping away,' or 'covering,' or ritual removal, of a substantive pollution contracted knowingly or unwittingly through contact with something that is defiling and 'unclean' (i.e. sacred and so taboo, as, for instance, a corpse). When it is the nature of the god, and consequently the processes dependent upon him, such as fertility, that are mainly involved, suitable offerings have to be made to secure the continuance of divine beneficence and set up a supernatural barrier against the forces of evil. On the other hand, when the condition of the worshipper is at fault, the ritual impurity, or contagious evil, contracted must be purged and removed by purification with water, propitiatory offerings or by the transference of the defilement to a 'sin-carrier'.

When a man is in a wrong relationship with the sacred order through pollution resulting from the infringement of a taboo, or some other ritual non-observance, he is 'desacralized' like the crops after a *sacrifice de sacralization* at the offering of the first-fruits. Therefore, he is liable to be a ready prey to the malevolent forces surrounding him, just as the harvest is consumed as soon as it ceases to be under divine ownership and protection. Thus, when fresh ground is broken, a new house is erected, trees are cut down or the products of the soil gathered, a fresh outpouring of vital energy liberated through a sacrificial offering is required as a protection against the spiritual beings associated with the place or object that is disturbed. Hence the practice of sprinkling blood or holy water on new land, new houses, and new wells which has survived into modern times. Curtiss records having witnessed the application of the blood of a goat on the cords of an Arab tent at Rubeibeh, and he gives a second-hand account of the pouring of sacrificial blood on the ground in the harvest fields, on the lintel of the house of a newly-married couple, at the laying of the foundations of a new government school at Kerak, and when the rail from Beirut to Damascus was begun.[1] Similarly, the regenerative properties of water have found expression in lustrations which have occupied a prominent place in propitiatory ritual and ceremonial atonement as a means of removing the uncleanness from a defiled person or object.

As impurity was carried away by running water, so animals were employed in expiation by scapegoats. In a Sumerian ritual-text describing an "incantation by means of the horned

[1] S. H. Curtiss, *Primitive Semitic Religion To-day*, pages 182ff.

wild goat", reference is made to the water-god, Ea, "Lord of the deep" (whence all rivers and springs were thought to take their origin) commanding his son Marduk to take a scapegoat to the king bound by a curse, and place it against his head to receive the "poisonous taboo into his mouth". On the reverse the goat is said to have been "unto the plain let loose," like the victim drawn by lot "for Azazel" in the Hebrew Day of Atonement observance on the tenth day of the seventh month (Lev. xvi). The king is referred to as "the son of his god," and, as Langdon has pointed out, he (the king) "communicates the sins of his people, the curse and ban of the devils, to the scapegoat by shooting it with an arrow".

The same attitude to sin and expiation lies behind the Jewish Day of Atonement ritual, where a very primitive rite was introduced into the levitical ceremonial after the time of Ezra in the middle of the fourth century B.C. The idea of atonement as a 'covering' of sin by the outpouring of the blood of the victim on behalf of sinners occupied a prominent place in the observances. A bullock and a ram were offered for the holy sanctuary, the tent of meeting, the altar and for all the people of the assembly, to remove the guilt incurred during the year. Two he-goats were then "set before Yahweh", and lots cast over them. The one selected for Yahweh was killed as a sin-offering, and the other "for Azazel" (probably a goat-demon of the desert waste) was "set alive before Yahweh" in order that atonement might be made over it before it was sent away into the wilderness (Lev. xvi, 3, 5-10).

According to a later and fuller account of the ceremony incorporated into the narrative (11-28), the blood of the bullock was sprinkled on the mercy-seat in the holy of holies, together with an offering of incense. The blood of the goat of the sin-offering was treated in the same way as an atonement for the people and the holy place, and at the end of the rite, when the high-priest had performed all his oblations, he laid his hands on the live goat, confessed over it all the sins of the congregation of Israel, and sent it away in charge of a man to discharge its burden of iniquity in a solitary land.

This done, the bullock and the goat were offered as sin-offerings and carried without the camp to be burned. Finally, a note has been added to this composite narrative to emphasize the purpose of the atonement made for the sanctuary, the tent of meeting, the altar, the priests and the people as a penitential annual purification when the nation must "afflict its soul and do no manner of work" (29-34) (cf. Lev. xxiii, 27-32).

Besides the crude ideas lying behind the blood-sprinkling rite, the cleansing and regenerative process was further assisted by offerings of incense and libations of holy water, all of which are clearly survivals of a primitive expiation ceremony going back to a very early phase in the history of custom and belief. It is true that a more ethical element was introduced under Rabbinical influence, and eventually the observance was interpreted mystically in Christian tradition in terms of the sacrifice of Christ and His eternal priesthood. But for our present purpose, its interest lies in the light it throws upon an earlier conception of evil as a substantive influence transferable from one person or object to another as a contagion, or miasma, removable by catharic agents and scapegoats. It was the blood of the victims that cleansed the defilement, while the goat 'for Azazel' was the vehicle by means of which the corruption was carried away into the desert. The animal in this type of atoning sacrifice is not itself a sacrificial victim destroyed to liberate life. Its function is that of carrying away the sin that hinders the free flow of divine beneficence. The ritual contagion has to be transferred to a human being, an animal or some inanimate object, unless it be removed by 'wiping off', or 'covering', by a purifying device that the "covenant with death be disannulled", and the bond of union with the source of life be re-established through a supernatural re-creative act, which is the essential meaning and purpose of the institution of sacrifice.

BIBLIOGRAPHY

Bevan, E. *Symbolism and Belief*. London, 1938.
Frazer, J. G. *The Golden Bough*. Pt. IV (The Dying God).

London, 1917. Pt. V. (Spirits of the Corn and of the Wild). 1912.

Freud, S. *Totem and Taboo.* London and New York, 1918.

Gray, G. B. *Sacrifice in the Old Testament.* Oxford, 1923.

Hooke, S. H. *Myth and Ritual.* Oxford, 1933.

Hubert, H., and Mauss, M. "Essai sur le sacrifice," *L'Année sociologique.* Vol. II. 1899.

Loisy, A. *Essai historique sur le Sacrifice.* Paris, 1920.

James, E. O. *Origin of Sacrifice.* London, 1933.

Marett, R. R. *Sacraments of Simple Folk.* Oxford, 1933.

Money-Kyrle, A. *The Meaning of Sacrifice.* London, 1930.

Oesterley, W. O. E. *Sacrifices in Ancient Israel.* London, 1937.

Smith, W. R. *Religion of the Semites.* 3rd Ed. London, 1927.

Westermarck, E. *Origin and Development of Moral Ideas.* London, 1906.

CHAPTER V

SPELL AND PRAYER

In the higher religions the approach to God through sacrifice and acts of communion usually leads up to, and is accompanied by, vocal expressions of corporate and individual needs and aspirations. In primitive society, on the other hand, the savage being essentially a man of action, he expresses by gestures rather than in words his inmost wishes and desires. For example, when rain, sunshine and the other conditions on which the harvest depends are urgently required, he does not keep 'rogation days' with greater zeal by engaging in corporate prayer for the blessing of God on the germinating crops. Rather he resorts to ceremonies which he believes actually produce results by liberating the forces that make for providential abundance, uttering spells, or 'words of power,' which state, command or invoke the desired aim and end.

The Sacred Utterance

The acquisition of articulate speech is generally thought by physical anthropologists to have been a very early endowment of the human race,[1] but it cannot be doubted that language was much more restricted than muscular movement when man first made his appearance on the earth, and at first it must have been confined for the most part to simple exclamations. In fact, it has been conjectured that the earliest entreaties were incoherent cries to the dead to 'come back' when they were laid to rest, though this suggestion hardly accords with the care bestowed upon the burial of the dead to prevent their return. Nevertheless, it is a common practice among primitive people to-day for invocations to be made during dances and mimetic gestures, and we know that dances were performed for magical purposes by masked figures in the Old Stone Age, since representations of this nature are depicted on the walls of the caves which are generally regarded as 'prehistoric sanctuaries'. Moreover, an engraving at Tiout Atlas, in North Africa, belonging to the Palæolithic culture phase known as Capsian, depicts a hunting scene in which an archer, apparently accompanied by a dog, is represented setting out to hunt ostriches. A woman with upstretched arms stands in an attitude which suggests that she was engaged in invocation or enchantment.[2]

Be this as it may, the origins of prayer have to be sought in words uttered in conjunction with sacred gestures directed to a transcendental source of potency for the purpose of giving expression to deep emotions and desires ; the incoherent cry of the human heart in time of need and stress. But it is often very difficult to distinguish prayer from spell, or magical formulæ in which the efficacy resides in the words spoken and the accompanying actions performed rather than in the divine being addressed, since the potency seems to lie in the actual utterance. Thus, the Iroquois in North America call praying

[1] Thus, both Sir Arthur Keith and Elliot Smith have assigned rudimentary speech on anatomical grounds to *Pithecanthropus*, the ape-man of Java, and to the "dawn man" (*Eoanthropus*) found at Piltdown in Sussex.

[2] H. R. Schmidt, *The Dawn of the Human Mind* (London, 1931), page 194f . . . 198. Fig. 94.

"laying down one's *orenda*," either because it is believed to be the act wherein a man surrenders his own power (*orenda* or *mana*) to a superior spiritual being, or, conversely, himself puts his own inherent power in operation. On the one hand, he may be "arrayed in his *orenda*" in order to obtain his desires, and, on the other hand, he may submit himself to an external source of strength in a prayerful attitude. In either case, *orenda*, which literally means 'song,' is a manifestation of power exercised from within or without through a supernatural agency capable of a magical or religious interpretation.

It was such potency that the Vedic priests wielded when, filled with divine efflatus, they sang their hymns and uttered what may be called the power of prayer, or *brahman ;* a neuter term originally comparable to *mana* signifying at once spell and sacred utterance. To be efficacious these hymns had to be composed with very great care and sung absolutely correctly, as the supernatural power lay within the words, as in any other spell. The gods, in fact, were as dependent upon them as they were upon the sacrificial offering, and while the vast majority of the hymns composing the Rig-Veda are persuasive and propitiatory rather than coercive, their purpose was to cultivate the goodwill of the gods, and so to induce them to bestow their benefits on their votaries in response to the service rendered in the cultus. Here the line which separates prayer from spell is very thin even though the hymns for the most part do not claim to influence the course of events without the intervention of divine beings.

In primitive society, as we have seen, the spoken word tends to be regarded as a charm, or incantation, exercising its own functions by virtue of its inherent potency. Thus, words used in a magical rite are chosen and pronounced with the greatest care and precision lest the spell should be broken by a slip of the tongue. The sounds may be onomatopœic, imitating the whistling of the wind, the rolling of thunder, the roar of the sea, and the noises made by animals ; or they may express certain emotional states associated with a desired end. The symptoms of a disease that the practitioner is endeavouring to cure or produce may be mentioned, or in the lethal formula the destruction of the victim will be pronounced. If the intention is to heal, word-pictures will be framed of health and strength by way of suggestion. In the economic sphere, the growing of plants, the approach of prey, or the arrival of fish in shoals may be described to bring about the actual occurrence in much the same way as hunting scenes were represented in prehistoric cave paintings with magical intent.

When the expression of the desire in action takes the form of words we are in the region of spell because the utterances are believed to achieve automatically their aim by the magic of the spoken word. This is apparent when sounds which have no meaning for the natives to-day are sung to promote the growth of vegetation and similar needs. The mere repetition of a sacred formula in these cases suffices to free the supernatural power inherent in the spell. On the other hand, when a particular divine being or class of spirits is addressed for a specific purpose this may be regarded as inchoate prayer, as, for instance when in the course of a dance during the initiation ceremonies among the Yuin tribe in South-east Australia, cries of 'Daramulun' are raised as an invocation to establish a relationship between the god of the mysteries and the initiates. But the exclamation "Come down rain!" sounds more like a command than an entreaty.

Prayers to High Gods

The use of the name of the All-Father in the Yuin rites is incidental to the act of dancing to obtain possession of the power that emanates from the High God, very much as in Central Australia the tribes derive their potency from the bull-roarer regarded as the sacramental sign of a Supreme Being, such as Twanyirika or Altjera. High Gods, however, are seldom the recipients of other than spontaneous and informal ejaculations as distinct from the systematic and systematized intercessions addressed to sentient spirits and divinities employed as mediators, or thought to be more directly responsive to human needs and entreaties. In their dignified seclusion from the world and its affairs, Supreme

Beings usually are beyond the reach of man except on very special occasions, such as before or after a hunt or battle, in times of drought or calamity, at the birth of a child, at the puberty of a daughter, at the death of a parent, or at some similar critical juncture, and then often through an intercessor in the capacity of a culture-hero or ancestor. Thus, for instance, among the Shilluk, normally Juok is approached through Nyakang, the semi-divine founder of the dynasty, but the Anuak tribe often offer to him certain dance songs in which they exclaim, "I pray God (Juok), the giver, God the protector ; I have taken God to me and have become fearful to my enemies so that they scarcely dare attack me." And the exclamation ends with the words, "I pray Juok alone, for he directs the spears ; spear-thrusts are of Juok !" Again, in interceding for a sick child the High God is petitioned by the Anuak thus : "Juok, you are great, you are the one who created me, I have no other. Juok, you are in the heavens, you are the only one, now my child is sick and you will grant me my desire".

In East Africa N'gai, the High God of the Eastern Bantu, is besought by the Akikuyu to give goats, sheep and children, while Dudley Kidd tells us that a tribe in Zululand invoked Unkulunkulu, the All-Father, for the recovery of the sick, though he agrees with Seligman and other observers among the Southern Bantu, that "this praying is rare because the Kafirs say that people prefer to pray to the Amatongo or spirits of people whom they have seen with their eyes rather than to Unkulunkulu, whom they have never seen".[1] A middle-aged native of the Wa Barwe tribe who had not had contact with missionaries affirmed that hunters when out hunting pray to Murungu (the Supreme Being) to let them hunt well. When people die suddenly their relatives pray to him to know the cause. In times of famine the chief assembles the tribe to dance the *mafue* (an ancient rain dance) before him "and Murungu answers with rain". If the ancestors fail to restore a sick man to health prayer is made to the High God "that he may get well", but except on these rather unusual occasions, "we do not pray to Murungu very much," the native

[1] *The Essential Kafir* (London, 1904), pages 98ff.

explained, "because he is too far away and there is no way to reach him. The *midzimu* (spirits of departed ancestors) pray to him because they can see a way to him and have reached to him. Generally we pray to them so that they can pray to Murungu". The Mashona peoples usually restrict their worship of their Supreme Being, Mwari, to once a year or twice in a very dry season. The women dance the *maque* and drink beer in the bush, where small huts are placed for the spirit of Mwari. They sing the same song that is sung by them when they are grinding the corn, which doubtless has a quasi-magical significance in relation to the production of the mealies. But the invocation for rain is made through the descendant of a deceased tribal chief, Nyakuwarwa, who communicates directly with the god by means of his own *tswikiro* (medium),[1] like the Wa Barwe *midzimo* in relation to Murungu.

In West Africa when a man marries, the Ibo and Kalabari of the Niger delta erect a shrine in the form of a rectangular basket for Chi, the Supreme Being. A medicine-man is brought to the house, and after sprinkling it with water as a purifying agent, and shaking his rattle, he invokes Chi as follows : "Behold your place set up for you ! Come, settle here and look after the household, both children and men. Come, take up your abode and protect the one who becomes your boy (or girl) to-day. You made this man (or woman). Keep near him and guard him all his life."[2] Therefore, although he lives far away in the sky, he is not disinterested in mankind and deigns to make his abode in the shrine erected in his honour as his local habitation at the request of his votaries. Conversely, the Pygmies beseech Mungu, the High God of the Bakango tribe, to depart when he appears in the sky in the form of the rainbow, or of the Ambelema snake "which turns into a rainbow when it climbs the sky".[3]

In North America, the Earthmaker, the Secondary Creator

[1] *Op. cit.*, page 289.

[2] P. A. Talbot, *Tribes of the Niger Delta* (London, 1932), pages 20f.

[3] P. Schebesta, *Among the Congo Pygmies* (London, 1933), pages 166f.

of the Winnebago, is thought never to hold direct communication with men, but in a myth that in all probability has undergone considerable re-interpretation, he is depicted as taking pity on the human race as the last of his creations, and decreeing that "whatever, from now on, the human beings ask of me and for which they offer tobacco, that I will not be able to refuse".[1] Here we have the conception of magical constraint transformed into the willing consent of the deity to grant requests in response to an offering. "Hearken Earthmaker, our Father, I am about to offer you tobacco. My ancestor concentrated his thoughts upon you. The blessings you bestowed upon him . . . those I ask of you directly . . . also that I may have no troubles in life".[2]

In the oldest myths of the Winnebago, as Dr. Radin has explained, there are two superior deities : the good spirit, Earthmaker, and the evil spirit, Hereshgumina, representing the respective chiefs of good and bad spirits. Originally, Earthmaker was a supernatural being in no way concerned with the creation of the world, or endowed with powers greater than Hereshgunina, but under shamanistic influence the ethical concept of a Creator-god was introduced together with other new elements, and in the Medicine Dance fused into a coherent whole in a conglomeration of spirit, culture hero, trickster, turtle, bladder, hare, sun, etc. Eventually, Earthmaker emerged as a full fledged Supreme Being who created all things of which the last and weakest was man. To rescue this pitiful 'two-legged walker' from his helplessness, he sent Hare to earth as the founder of the Medicine Dance and the intermediary who is to lead man to the presence of Earthmaker.[3]

If this is substantially a correct analysis of the transformation of the figure of Earthmaker, it illustrates the way in which a remote and undefined religious concept that finds expression in the idea of a Supreme Being, has been combined by a religious formulator with defined notions concerning the

[1] Radin, 37*th Report of Bureau of American Ethnology* (Washington, 1923), pages 478ff.

[2] Radin, *Monotheism among Primitive Peoples* (London, 1924), page 43.

[3] 37*th R.B.A.E.*, pages 350ff.

attributes of human beings and spiritual entities to whom prayers and offerings are made in an organized cultus. In the most primitive states of culture prayer primarily is confined to inchoate utterances, mainly in the form of ejaculations or simple petitions made to vaguely conceived High Gods, or to any sacred object or entity in possession of *mana*. The only explicit prayer addressed to an Australian All-Father, for instance, is that recorded by Mrs. Langloh Parker who affirms that at initiation ceremonies the oldest tribesman present invoked Baiame to give the people long life. At funerals the spirit of the deceased was commended to him with the request that the dead man might enter the sky world as he had kept the Boorah laws. In times of drought an orphan ran out when the clouds were overhead, and looking up cried, "Water come down!" Anything in the nature of formal and set prayers at regular intervals, however, seemed to the Euahlayi tribe "a foolishness and an insult" to Baiame. Since "he knows, why weary him with repetition disturbing the rest he enjoys after his earth labours?"[1]

At a relatively higher cultural level, Sir A. B. Ellis tells us that among the Ewe-speaking peoples of West Africa "prayers that are addressed to the gods are not in any stereotyped form, but worshippers ask for what they want in natural language, with a certain amount of adulation, just as they might prefer a petition to a chief".[2] Sometimes primitive prayers are preceded by a sacred call or ejaculation, such as the Todas cry, 'On' uttered at regular intervals throughout the daily ritual,[3] or the Delaware 'Ho-o-o!' raised twelve times at the end of each day's ceremonies in connexion with their annual Thanksgiving rite.[4] These sounds seem to be devoid of any conceptual connotation, and, as Otto suggests, they may be the means by which numinous feeling is

[1] *The Euahlayi Tribe* (London, 1900), pages 8f, 79, 89.

[2] *Ewe-speaking Peoples of West Africa* (London, 1890), page 80.

[3] Rivers, *The Todas* (London, 1906), page 65.

[4] F. G. Speck, *Publications of the Pennsylvania Historical Commission* (Harrisburg, 1931), Vol. II, page 145.

articulated,[1] though doubtless they also represent an attempt to attract the attention of the deity and invoke his aid, as in the cry, "O Baal, hear us !" Similarly, the power in the name of a god is called forth by giving utterance to it, as in the repetition of Amida-Buddha in the Jodo sect in Japan where those who engage in the exercise are thought to be brought within the natural activity of Amida, the essence of all things and the infinite light penetrating all regions of the universe. Thereby they obtain freedom from passion and suffering.

Acted Prayers

More explicit than the words spoken are the actions performed when man is prone to dramatize his desires and make his needs known to a transcendent source of strength by mimetic rites, which are virtually acted prayers. In the most primitive states of culture even ejaculations are seldom made without some corresponding gesture, and generally the more articulate prayers are embedded in a rite. Writing of the Tarahumare Indians, Lumholtz says, "the favour of the gods may be won by what for want of a better term may be called dancing, but what in reality is a series of monotonous movements, a kind of rhythmical exercise, kept up sometimes for two nights. By dint of such hard work they think to prevail upon the gods to grant their prayers. The dancing is accompanied by the song of the shaman. . . . He invokes the aid of all the animals, mentioning each by name and calls on them, especially the deer and the rabbit, to multiply that the people may have plenty to eat. As a matter of fact the Tarahumares assert that the dances have been taught them by the animals . . . and as the gods grant the prayers of the deer expressed in antics and dances, and of the turkey in his curious playing, by sending the rain, they easily infer that to please the gods they, too, must dance as the deer and play as the turkey. Dancing, in fact, not only expresses prayers for rain and life, but also petitions to the gods to ward off evil in any shape, as diseases of man, beast or crops. . . .

[1] *The Idea of the Holy*, page 197.

By dancing and with the tesvino (native beer) they express all their wants to the gods, or, as a Tarahumare told me 'we pray by dancing and the gourd'."[1] This, in fact, bears out Marett s contention that "from dance to prayer might almost be said to sum up the history of religion regarded as a mode of human self-expression".[2]

So long as prayer retains its original spontaneity it occupies a subordinate position in the religious life of the community, and is completely overshadowed by the organized cultus. While it is directed to every type of divine being and sacred object from Supreme Deities to human artefacts, and touches the life of primitive man at many points, it is confined mainly to invocation for material needs and benefits; and, as has been observed, it is offered principally at critical junctures in the career of the individual, or at the seasonal gatherings of the tribe. As the ancient Ainu hunters used to address petitions to their poisoned arrows, which they thought were "invested with life; heard prayers, and did as they were requested", so fishermen entreat the good will of their nets in order to ensure a successful catch on the assumption that the nets report the petition to the fish.

Invocation of Spirits and Gods

Invocations for specific and urgent desires are offered, however, principally to ancestors, animistic spirits and departmental gods whose function it is to control particular operations. Thus, the Veddas in times of calamity erect an arrow in the ground and dance round it calling upon the ancestors who watch over their welfare to come to their aid:

> "My departed one, my departed one,
> My God! Where are you wandering?"

This invocation appears to be used on all occasions when the intervention of the guardian spirit is required. Not infrequently the ghosts of the dead are thought to be vindictive,

[1] C. Lumholtz, *Unknown Mexico* (London, 1903), Vol. I, pages 330f, 332, 340, 521.

[2] *Heads, Hearts and Hands in Human Evolution*, page 96.

and, consequently, the relatives can never be certain how they will behave. Any omission of the reverence and respect due to them will be visited on the head of the descendants in some manner or another. Therefore, at times of misfortune the Ba-Ila, for example, turn to their ancestors with prayers such as the following :

> Tsu ! If it be thou, O leave me alone, that I may get well. What is it thou requirest ? See, here is tobacco, here is water, here is beer. Leave me alone that I may enjoy myself."

In Bechuanaland when a drought is severe a man takes his wooden milk-pail, the thong used for tying his cow's legs before milking, his shepherd's crook, and an ox-bone, and cries aloud as he holds them over his ancestor's grave : "Have compassion upon us, and let these things still be of use !"

That human beings in times of danger and distress should seek the aid of deified ghosts of the dead is a natural consequence of the intimate relations existing between them. Thus, according to Codrington, "the *tataro* of the Banks Islands, which may be called a prayer, is strictly an invocation of the dead", and he thinks that the appeal to two *vui*, Kwat and Marawa, regarded by him as non-human spiritual beings, is not a *tataro*.[1] But it may be an adaptation of the practice of praying to ghosts (*tamate*) for help in similar circumstances, since prayers for succour were made properly to a deceased father, uncle or grandfather. This would seem to indicate that the worship of *tamate* preceded that of *vui*, and that subsequently Kwat and Marawa were placed with *tamate* as helpers and deliverers to be approached indirectly in contrast to the direct and personal appeals to the ghosts of the dead. Taking the Melanesian evidence as a whole, the cultus of the spirits (*vui*) is a specialized discipline confined almost entirely to matters connected with material prosperity and particular events or objects (e.g. war, snake worship, taboo, banito-fishing, stones), while that of the *tamate* was concerned with bodily welfare.

The powers and functions of localized spirits and divinities

[1] *The Melanesians*, pages 146, 148, 150, 152.

are usually so limited, and the entities themselves so numerous, that, like the Roman *numena*, they are but dimly conceived and very hard to invoke with certainty and security. They are frequently unnamed except in general terms, such as *mura-mura*, or *vui*, and unseen save for the symbol of their abode ; a tree, stone, animal or other material object. To them petitions may be addressed on occasions so that, for instance, no Herero passes by a sacred tree without at least laying a stone at its foot with the words, "Hail ! Father !" But normally it is to the thing itself (or its *mana*), or the deified ancestors, the guardian spirits and the departmental gods, and such Supreme Beings as have become entangled with the affairs of this world, that man turns with specific requests, or to offer acts of praise for benefits received. Warriors call upon the gods of war, merchants on the divine patrons of the market-place, women on the bestowers of fertility, and, in fact, in almost every aspect of human activity from the cradle to the grave, and the hunting grounds to the city-state, in daily work and business, or in times of emergency, calamity or seasonal change, a special divinity or supernatural efficacy controlling the operations in question is invoked. Villages, hamlets, cities and provinces, as well as crafts and occupations, have their own tutelary gods and spirits, as in later times they have acquired patron saints and local madonnas, and to these prayers and supplications are offered on appropriate occasions. Among the ancient Romans the spirits of the farm and fields (Lares) were worshipped jointly by the owners of adjoining properties at the festival of Compitalia in January, and one of these spirits became especially attached to the house where he took his place with the other household gods as the Lar familiaris, or guardian, watching over its fortunes, just as every man had his Genius.

The ancient belief that a child was formed in its mother's womb from the blood that was shed during gestation, led to the placenta being regarded as a reserve of vital material, or soul-substance, which gives to the human body life, strength and health, and is intimately related to the welfare of the individual. Thus, it acquired the reputation of being the child's secret helper, or protecting genius throughout life, a kind of twin brother, analogous to the totem or tutelary spirit—the ally bound to the man by a blood-bond. Hence the equation of the Genius which every Roman man was thought to possess with the virile powers of the male which make for the continuance of the family, personified as an indwelling spirit, worshipped on his birthday. To the Genius of the Paterfamilias the prayers of the household were directed, as to the spirit of a *living* ancestor in whom the hopes of the family are centred. From this practice the worship of the Genius of the Emperor on the Palatine eventually emerged as the supreme act of devotion in the cultus of the Empire in conjunction with that of the Dea Roma.

All these localized and individualized divinities are restricted to their own circumscribed sphere of influence over the particular processes, places or people they control. Within their own province they are supreme, or at any rate a power to be reckoned with. Therefore, they are invoked in connexion with the matters with which they are primarily concerned, though as the reputation of a god increases, or he is raised to higher rank in the pantheon as a result of the growth in importance of the city or country over which he presides, his power extends as his domain is enlarged. This has the reciprocal effect of making him the recipient of prayers for a great variety of requests, till at length he absorbs all the attributes of all the gods, as in the case of Marduk when his city, Babylon, became the capital.

So long as attention is concentrated on the problems of physical life, how to obtain food, reproduce the species and survive in the midst of so many and great dangers, prayer seldom rises above the material plane of everyday needs and mundane affairs, whether it consists of inchoate cries for help or organized supplication to specific divinities. The varieties of the objects and purpose for which requests are made correspond to the evaluation of the conception of Deity and the nature of the spiritual experience of the people concerned. Prayer for moral values is alien to primitive society, and is almost entirely non-existent in the religions of the ancient civilizations prior to the rise of ethical thought in Greece and in Israel. A Thonga father at the time of the marriage of his daughter prays that she may be "happy, good and just," and a Baganda leather-thrower resorting to divination exclaims, "O Mwanga, my master, give the right decision in this matter". But while it is possible to read into such statements an ethical significance, it has to be remembered that the primitive interpretation of 'goodness' is that of beneficence and material prosperity. Indeed, in primitive society, as we have seen, the nearer a god becomes to an ethical Supreme Being the less usually is he approached in prayer.

Prayer and Confession

The primitive conception of right and wrong being that of ritual holiness, the Indian in Mexico, for example, never asks his god to forgive him whatever sin he may have committed. . . . The only wrong towards the gods of which he may consider himself guilty is that he does not dance enough. For this offence he asks pardon. Whatever bad thoughts or actions towards man he may have on his conscience are settled between himself and the person concerned. Nevertheless, before seeking hikuli, a small cactus which when eaten produces ecstasy, confession is made to Grandfather Fire first by the women and then by the men. Similarly, in Peru confession was a public duty in Inca society arising out of the belief that the sins of the individual were liable to have disastrous consequences on the whole community, as in Israel in the days of Achan. Each penitent prostrated before the confessor, who was a kind of priest or diviner, and then made a full disclosure of his sins, which were partly crimes against his neighbour's life and property, partly offences of a religious nature, such as failure to reverence the Sun and to keep the appointed festivals, and also moral lapses including adultery and fornication. The confessor exhorted the penitent to pursue a correct mode of life and gave him a few light strokes on the back with a small stone tied to a string. Thereupon both spat on a bundle of esparto grass, and the priest spoke to his gods accursing the sins.

This having been done, the bundle was thrown into the river, and prayers were made to the gods that they would take the sins down into the abyss and hide them for ever.

Making due allowance for the fact that this record came in the first instance from an anonymous Jesuit who, as Karsten suggests, doubtless saw the rite "with Catholic eyes", in the relatively advanced state of culture represented by the Inca kingdom in Peru, there is every reason to think that confession was an established institution involving some realization of a higher conception of sin and righteousness and their moral implications. But everywhere prayer of this nature is a late development arising out of the earlier notion of ritual holiness and cathartic purification when the agent sufficed to purge or carry away the sin. In primitive cults and the religions of antiquity prior to the rise of ethical concepts, the deep sense of sinfulness, humility and contrition, characteristic of Hebrew and Christian prayers, never finds expression, even though on occasions it may be latent. The difference between right and wrong is perceived at all levels of culture, but it is not until the essential righteousness of Deity is established as an ethical attribute that repentance emerges. It is then, and only then, that confession becomes an integral element in prayer as "the sacrifice of the lips" and a declaration of a contrite heart in the presence of a holy God, instead of a repudiation of errors committed wittingly or unwittingly exorcised by ritual devices.

Prayer and Thanksgiving

Again, while the primitive is not devoid of a sense of gratitude for benefits received or dangers averted, he does not express his emotions in formal thanksgivings. As Dr. Hopkins says, "when the fear is stilled and the hope gratified the savage rejoices, but to offer thanks to the spiritual powers for their favour is as rare as to thank a man for service".[1] An exception to the rule, if the episode has been correctly described, is at the eating of the new yams among the Onitsha on the Niger river, when the medicine man takes a yam after

[1] Hopkins, *History of Religions* (New York, 1928), page 95.

it has been roasted, scrapes it into a sort of meal, and divides it into halves. He then takes one piece and places it on the lips of the person who is going to eat the new yam. The eater blows up the steam from the hot yam, and puts it into his mouth saying, "I thank god for being permitted to eat the new yam". But the absence of a special word for 'thanks' in many native languages shows that the idea of thankfulness is not prominent in primitive society, though it may be a fact, as Heiler suggests, that acknowledgment for gifts from a beneficent Providence is to be found in such a phrase as "thou hast done it". The name of the god is invoked and the thing received is specified thus : "O Waka, thou hast given me this buffalo, this honey, this wine". Such, he thinks, is the prayer of thanksgiving of the African Pygmy. Or, again, a Khond, when he has escaped a great danger, says, "Thou hast rescued me, O God," and before drinking wine an Ainu salutes his divinity thanking him for his kindness.[1]

While a sense of gratitude seems to be latent in prayers or assertions of this kind, arising out of a consciousness of dependence on higher powers for daily needs and special protection in times of trouble, their immediate purpose is to ensure the future favour of the god. Thus, first-fruit rituals and harvest 'thanksgivings' are primarily utilitarian inasmuch as they are held to promote the fertility of the crops during the forthcoming season, though not infrequently they take the form of an honorarium in recognition of providential bounty, and are accompanied by expressions of gratitude, as in the annual Thanksgiving Ceremony of the Lenape-Delawares in North America, when the high priest prays as follows :

> I am thankful, O thou Great Spirit, that we have been spared to live until now to purify with cedar smoke this our House, because that has always been the rule in the ancient world since the beginning of creation. When any one thinks of his children, how fortunate it is to see them enjoy good health! And this is the cause of a feeling of happiness, when we consider how greatly we are blessed by the benevolence of our

[1] Heiler, *Prayer*, pages 6, 38f.

> Father, the Great Spirit. And we can also feel the great strength of him, our Grandfather. First to whom we give pleasure when we purify him and take care of him, and when we feed him with this cedar. All of this together we offer in esteem to him, our Grandfather, because he has compassion, when he sees how pitifully we behave while we are pleading with all the mannitto above, as they were created, and with all those here on earth. Give us everything, our Father, that we ask of you, Great Spirit, even the Creator. [1]

Here the eucharistic conception of prayer is struggling to find expression in relation to a more lofty and intimate attitude towards Deity, regarded as a beneficent bestower of his bountiful gifts on mankind in response to the petitions and offerings of his people. Although this cannot be taken as typical of a genuinely primitive mode of address to the higher powers, germinal feelings of gratitude may never have been entirely absent in man's reverential approach to the ultimate source of his life and general well-being.

BIBLIOGRAPHY

Clodd, E. *Magic in Names*. London, 1920.

Farnell, L. R. *Evolution of Religion*. London, 1905.

Frazer, J. G. *Golden Bough*. Pt. I (Magic Art). London, 1914.

Harrison, J. E. *Ancient Art and Ritual*. London, 1913.

Heiler, F. *Prayer*. Oxford, 1937.

Marett, R. R. *The Threshold of Religion*. London, 1914.

Radin, P. *Primitive Religion*. London, 1938.

Tylor, E. B. *Primitive Culture*. 4th Edition. London, 1903. Vol. II.

CHAPTER VI

THE CULT OF THE DEAD AND IMMORTALITY

THE ritual organization as the most stable and permanent element in primitive society finds its ultimate goal in the

[1] Speck, *Publications of the Pennsylvanian Historical Commission* (Harrisbury, 1931), Vol. II, page 75.

supreme and final crisis in the life of the individual, namely his departure out of this world. From the cradle to the grave human existence consists of a succession of transitions, comparable to the cycle of the seasons in nature, in which the process of decay and regeneration is exemplified. All life it seems is in a state of flux, "never continuing in one stay"; a perpetual dying to be born again. So at birth, adolescence, marriage and death, as at seed-time and harvest and the turn of the year, a series of *rites de passage*, as the French writer Van Gennep calls them, has to be celebrated to ensure providential protection and aid against the forces of evil rampant at these critical junctures, and to obtain a fresh outpouring of life and power.

Transitional Rites

This transitional ritual from life to death or from death to life, arising out of a tension of instinctive need, emotional stress, and unsatisfied desire, involves first of all a separation from the former mode of existence, followed by a real or simulated death and rebirth, leading on to an installation in the new condition. Thus, at birth the spirit-child as a denizen from the 'beyond' has to be purified and purged from its sacred contagion, reborn into this world and installed as a member of a particular family. Similarly, at the time of initiation, the adolescent has to put away childish things, undergo tests of endurance, prolonged fasting and a period of seclusion before he can be reborn into the adult fellowship of the tribe and given his official status in society.

So death being the gateway to the other world, the same cycle of rites have to be performed to enable the deceased to break away from his terrestrial existence and its associations, pass successfully through the dark and dangerous "valley of the shadow", and be safely and securely launched on his new career beyond the grave. Thus, the idea of immortality has arisen not so much from speculations about a separable soul and phantoms of the living, as from this ritual organization of which it is the natural corollary. For the primitive mind ever-renewing life is the normal sequence of events, and death is merely an intrusion, caused by violence, black magic, or supernatural vengeance of some kind, which must be overcome by a fresh gift of revitalizing energy, as in the case of the ceremonial interments found in the caves of the Old Stone Age, where the corpse was surrounded with red ochre as a substitute for blood, and with other life-giving objects such as shells; or by the performance of transitional rites. Consequently, it is the funeral ritual that determines the condition of the dead in the hereafter. Around these ceremonies the doctrine of immortality has developed.

Fear of the Dead

It is not surprising, therefore, that the worst fate that can befall a man in this state of society is to be unburied, or to have an inadequate funeral; a view that still lingers on in the lower strata of modern communities. Just as an unwanted child is thought to return whence it comes by the omission of the birth-rites—for true birth requires the completion of all the installation observances—so re-admission to the spirit-world is dependent upon a similar initiatory ritual. Hence the vengeance of revengeful ghosts meted out to relatives who fail in this all-important duty, and the precautions taken to prevent the return of spirits of the dead who, for some reason or another, have a grudge against the living. If this is most apparent in the case of those whose obsequies have been omitted or imperfectly fulfilled, it applies also to anyone who has died a violent death, passed out of the world prematurely, or even sometimes to the unmarried and the childless.

Various methods have been devised to deal with this precarious situation, ranging from the destruction of the belongings of the deceased to carrying the corpse by devious ways to the place of burial, binding, blindfolding or mutilating it, disguising the mourners and relatives, making noises, unpleasant odours and brandishing weapons to scare away the ghost. When the funeral rites are adequately and punctiliously performed the danger of unwelcome visitations is minimized, and this doubtless explains the relative absence of fear of the dead in Ancient Egypt, where the most elaborate methods were employed to render the body immortal. Therefore, it would seem that while fear unquestionably was and is the motive behind many of the customs observed at the time of a death, the main purpose of the cult of the dead is positive rather than negative. It is to install the departed into the next life, thereby rendering the spirit harmless to the survivors and at peace with itself, and also to remove the dangerous sacred contagion surrounding the corpse and those who have to come into intimate contact with it, or who are near of kin to the deceased. The general attitude displayed towards a dead body, in fact, is that usually adopted by primitive people in the presence of any sacred object; namely, a combination of the fear, respect and reverence shown to a being who is half-god and half-devil, or perhaps god and devil by turns.

The Last Rites

Before the actual dissolution occurs, the nearest relatives, and sometimes the whole community, foregather to perform 'the last rites'. These usually consist in a series of ceremonies designed to sever the passing soul from its earthly connexions and environment and to fortify it for its final conflict and passage to the next abode. As this journey usually involves a struggle with hostile forces, the relatives and mourners have to assist in driving away the supernatural foes. This may take the form of a ritual combat in which they rush about cutting themselves with knives, battering one another with clubs and making unearthly noises (wailing, beating drums, etc.), thereby performing a dual function: (1) scaring malign influences, and (2) showing seemly grief and consternation at the approaching demise, gratifying, it is hoped, to the spirit who will be both protected and mollified, and so disinclined to return and molest them.

Meanwhile provision is prepared for the journey, and as soon as the death has occurred, the body is washed, anointed and clothed in new garments; or it may be simply rolled up in a rug and lightly corded before being taken to the place of burial amid a renewal of loud lamentation. Conventionalized wailing, in fact, is the characteristic feature of the proceedings everywhere, often accompanied by smearing the bodies of the mourners with pipe-clay, shaving their heads, or the wearing of distinctive garments. Sometimes blood-letting ensues to revivify the corpse, and on occasions portions of it may be consumed sacramentally to imbibe its qualities or to establish a bond of union with it.

The Disposal of the Body

When mortuary rites of this nature have been duly performed the actual burial follows. This may take a great variety of forms, such as inhumation in a grave dug in the ground, exposure of the corpse on a platform raised on a scaffold, or concealing it in branches of trees or in a cave, setting it adrift in a canoe, preserving the tissues by some process of mummification or destroying them by cremation. The choice of a method of disposal frequently is determined by the status in society of the deceased. Thus, raised burial or cremation may be reserved for chiefs and warriors while inhumation suffices for commoners. In Polynesia, for example, the tribe tends to bisect at death so that in Tahiti the nobility and members of the great Areioi secret society, together with the chief, go to a paradise on the top of a mountain in Raiates (which in all probability originally was a celestial heaven and the home of the ancient gods and heroes), while the rest of the people pass to the underworld. Similarly, in Hawaii there is a vague belief that chiefs are conducted to the sky (*Meru*) by the "Eyeball of the Sun" before they are reborn on earth. The references to a celestial hereafter for rulers in New Zealand may have been influenced by Christianity, but, nevertheless, in some tribes it was held that the souls of chiefs and *Tohungas* (priests) at least ascended to heaven (*Rangi*) to their Sky Father Parent. This is supported by evidence collected in the South Island where incantations were sung by the *tohunga* at the burial of rulers and priests to assist the soul to ascend, or, in the case of commoners, to help it to descend to Po, the "Place of Night". In their ascent the rulers passed through different heavens till they reached at the tenth stage the residence of the gods, and so attained their complete deification.

In most of Eastern Australia and parts of the West and North-west, where mummification and secondary burial after exposure in trees or on platforms are practised for the most distinguished members of the community, their final destination is the sky, whither the culture-heroes ascended in the Golden Age at the end of their earthly sojourn. Thus, among the native tribes of Queensland and the Darling-Murray basins, men of eminence, such as warriors, are disembowelled after death and the body is anointed with fat and red ochre and desiccated over a fire, or in the sun. It is then packed, bound up, painted and made into a bundle. This is carried about for months by the mourners from camp to camp until all the rites have been duly performed and the death avenged. Finally it is interred or cremated, exposed on a platform, or in the hollow of a tree.[1] Sometimes preservation follows a previous interment and disinterment, or the bundle may consist merely of the bones and the dried skin when the flesh has been consumed at a cannibalistic feast.[2]

The practice of eating certain parts of the body by prescribed relatives is a mark of distinction reserved for persons of special worth in society whose particular qualities are thereby conveyed sacramentally to the survivors. Furthermore, it is a quick method of preparing the bundle, leaving intact the more permanent parts of the mortal remains. In Australia, however, the body is only preserved for a specific period, viz., for the duration of the mourning ceremonies and until the death has been avenged. It is then cremated, exposed or interred, having served its purpose as the integument of the spirit. Thus, it would seem that mummification in this region is an intermediate phase in the final liberation of the real entity that survives the dissolution, connected primarily with the funerary ritual of persons of distinction whose bodies cannot be summarily disposed of, as in the

[1] W. E. Roth, North Queensland Ethnography, Bulletin 9, *Records of the Australian Museum*, Vol. VI, 1907, page 393.

[2] A. P. Elkin, *The Australian Aborigines* (Sydney and London, 1938), page 249.

case of the uninitiated and lesser members of the tribe. Originally, however, the practice may have arisen from a desire to preserve the dead indefinitely.

Mummification

It was in Ancient Egypt, of course, that this conception of immortality found its most complete expression in the elaborate ritual of mummification and its complex psychology of the human organism as a series of "coverings" of which the last was the material body. At death it was the duty of the embalmers to render the tissues imperishable and to restore the likeness of the deceased, while the priests had to reconstitute the mental faculties and revivify the mummy by the aid of water, incense, and similar life-giving agents and potent amulets. By this 'Opening of the Mouth' ceremony the individual became a re-created 'living soul' (*ba*) and was given strength and ability to confront successfully his spiritual adversaries beyond the grave.[1]

This elaborate method of attaining immortality by a series of mechanical and magical operations was beyond the powers of peoples in a primitive state of culture, and indeed it proved too expensive in Egypt to be within the reach of any but the ruling classes. Commoners do not appear to have been much concerned with this aspect of the cult of the dead and its psychology, and they continued to regard the grave as the approach to the underworld ruled over by Osiris. And even in more exalted circles portrait statues of the deceased frequently were concealed in secret chambers to serve as a body for the disembodied individual, if and when its imperfectly preserved mummy decayed. Thus, images and masks tended to become a part of the funerary equipment, and were treated in the same way as the mummified remains. To transform them into a living soul they were re-animated by libations of Nile water, censings, and touching the eyes, nose and ears with a copper chisel. So intimate in fact was the connexion between the statue and the body that the sculptor was called "he who makes to live" (*s'nh*), inasmuch as it was as a result

[1] W. R. Dawson, *Journal of Egyptian Archaeology*, XIII, Parts I, II, 1927, pages 40ff.

of his labours that the dead had a permanent abode in this world.

Behind these elaborations lay a primitive cultus which has found expression in various attempts to preserve the mortal remains, or their surrogate, and ultimately to subordinate them to another purpose far removed from their original intention, viz., to liberate the spirit from the body. Frequently only the skin and the bones are kept, though sometimes the empty spaces are filled with packing of white sand or some other desiccating substance. In the New World, in Virginia, for example, the skin, which had been slit down the back, was then sewed up in order that the body might present its natural appearance. To prevent it from shrinking or corrupting it was oiled, and the flesh was also thoroughly dried, sewed up in a basket and set at the feet of the corpse. The bones were similarly dried in the sun before they were put into the skin again and the cavities were filled with fine sand. A more elaborate method was adopted by the Aleutian islanders who embalmed the bodies of chiefs with dried moss and grass, and clothed them in their best attire before burying them in a sitting posture in a strong box with their weapons and instruments. The mummified remains of a chief found in a cave by Captain Hemming in the island of Kagamale were covered with a fine skin of sea-otter (always a mark of distinction in burials in this region), and enclosed in a basket-like structure overlaid with a fish-net.[1]

In the South-western region of North America similar mummified remains have been discovered at the Mesa Verde ruins, San Juan, wrapped in the flexed position in a kind of mat made of osiers tied together by long cords of yucca. Over the head a bowl had been placed, and near by another mummy with the head covered with a skin cap and the feet in moccasins. The corpse was wrapped in a net of cords held together with strands of yucca leaf and wound with strips of hide. Under the mummy lay a mat of withes, while below the head was a block of wood. A similar mat had

[1] It is not improbable that these methods were diffused from Asia where among the Ainu anal evisceration was also practised and the body was dried in the sun.

been spread over the body. In front of the head stood a well-preserved basket half full of maize meal, and beside it lay a small ladle or spoon.[1] In this area a number of natural mummies have been found. In the Basket-Maker caves of North-eastern Arizona the bodies were sometimes wrapped in blankets and woven clothes and strung together in the contracted position in the form of mummy-bundles, as in Australia, resembling those depicted in the Mexican manuscripts.

Thus, in Codex Magliabecchiano (sheet 60) in the Biblioteca Nazionale, Florence, a swathed figure standing upright is represented having a band with a plate of turquoise-mosaic on the head. The hair is decorated with cotton-tails and feathers and a banner of the god, Uitzilopochtli, also adorns the head. Beside it stands a hairless dog, and in front gifts to be presented to Mictlantecutli, the god of the underworld.[2] Similar bundles are illustrated in varying degrees of formation in the Codex Borbonicus (sheet 28) and in the Sahagun manuscript in the Biblioteca del Palacio, Madrid, while the Maya symbol of the so-called "Heavenly Shield" seems to contain two mummy-bundles on either side of the central figure.[3]

From these representations it would appear that in the Mexican plateau mummification was widely practised in ancient times, and its survival in Southern New Mexico is revealed in the desiccated bodies brought to light in the caves of Arizona and in the Lower Mimbres valley. In the Eastern States in the saltpetre caves of Kentucky, mummies wrapped in deer skins and surrounded by utensils, beads, feathers and other ornaments have been found. While in none of these natural mummies was there any sign of evisceration, the fact that the bodies invariably had been clad and ornamented with great care, or mudded into cists, shows that they had

[1] G. Nordenskïold, *The Cliff Dwellers of the Mesa Verde* (Stockholm, 1893), pages 38ff.

[2] Z. Nuttall, *The Book of the Life of the Ancient Mexicans* (Berkeley, 1903), pages 54ff. Duc de Loubat, *Codex Magliabecchiano*, 13, 3 (Rome, 1904).

[3] Brinton, *Mayan Hieroglyphics* (Boston, 1895), page 107f.

been placed in the caves deliberately for the purpose of preserving the mortal remains.

Natural desiccation, however, is necessarily restricted to regions where the means are available. Elsewhere the body frequently is dried artificially over a slow fire, as in Australia or in Nicaragua, where a chief after death is wrapped in clothes and suspended by ropes before a fire till the corpse is baked to dryness. When it has been preserved for a year it is taken to the market-place and burned in the belief that the smoke goes "to the place where the dead man's soul is". In Florida, where the dead are said to have been clothed in rich coverings, dried before a fire and placed in a niche in a cave, fragments of partly incinerated human bones have been discovered in a mound at Cade's Point near Santa Fe Lake in association with other skulls showing no signs of the action of fire. Similarly, blackened human bones embedded in charcoal have been found in native cemeteries in British Honduras, and east of the Mississippi.

Cremation

It is not improbable that this practice of drying the corpse over a fire was one of the contributory causes of cremation, though, of course, there may have been many other reasons for committing a body to the flames. The remains of warriors killed in battle, for example, sometimes have been reduced to ashes for the sake of convenience in carrying home the relics to be deposited in the sepulchres of their ancestors. Or, again, when the dead are feared cremation is often adopted to prevent the return of the malicious ghost, and stillborn or unwanted infants as of no value are disposed of by this means. In New Zealand, in open country, in the absence of any suitable places for the permanent preservation of the bones, after exhumation they are collected from the trees or grave where they have been temporarily lodged, and burned at the conclusion of the funeral feast, presumably to prevent desecration.

Nevertheless, the fact that preservation and cremation, though contrary in nature, are so intimately related in practice over a wide area, suggests that a deeper significance lay behind the custom of burning bodies that have been previously embalmed, desiccated or mummified, especially as frequently the incinerated remains are subsequently buried. Thus, among the Aztecs the corpse was washed in aromatic water before it was placed on the pyre. It is not improbable that this was a survival of the practice of mummification since in the series of pictures depicting the Michoacan funeral rites in the 16th century Spanish MS., *Relación de los ceremonios y ritos de Michoacan*, the actual mummy is represented swathed in rolls of cotton and carried on the heads of four bearers to be consumed on a blazing fire. Similarly, in a painting at Chichen Itza in Yucatan, the preparation of a corpse for cremation is shown with the body opened to extract the heart and viscera, which, after being charred, are to be preserved in a stone urn with cinnabar.[1]

From a remote period fire has been regarded as a spiritualizing agent, and for this reason sacrificial offerings have been burnt to liberate the vital essence. Thus, in the Solomon Islands it is held that when an offering is destroyed in the fire the spirit can eat it, and the Semitic custom of passing children through the fire was prompted apparently by the belief that fire releases all things from "the bondage of corruption", converting "our material nature into an immaterial".[2] Moreover, it had the property of conferring the gifts of immortality on mortals, as is demonstrated in the story of Isis in the house of the king of Byblus, of Demeter in the house of the king of Eleusis, of Thetis in the house of her husband Peleus, where royal infants were made immortal by burning them in the fire. In Brahmanic ritual in India, fire is the vehicle by which each organ and attribute is conveyed to the corresponding part of the universe, and "three sacred fires were kindled to assist the soul in its ascent to the sky".[3] Similarly, in a more primitive state of culture,

[1] A. le Plongeon, *Queen Moo and the Egyptian Sphinx* (London, 1896), page 138.

[2] Iamblicus, *De Mysteriis*, 12.

[3] Monier-Williams, *Brahmanism and Hinduism* (London, 1887), page 283f.

the soul in the New Hebrides is thought to rise to the sun by means of the fire kindled at the grave.[1]

It cannot be maintained that cremation always has been associated with the idea of a celestial hereafter, but when this has been the case, very frequently the rite had been adopted for the purpose of liberating the spirit and transferring it to the sky. In California, for instance, the ashes of the corpse were scattered in the air to give the disembodied spirit wings so that it mounts up to hover for ever in the upper regions, like Herakles who, in the Tyrian version of the legend, is said to have ascended in the smoke of his funeral pyre. The Diegueño, who lived formerly in and around San Diego, made effigies of eagle feathers, matting and cloth, at the fiesta of the images, which were supposed to contain the spirit of the deceased. The face was carefully constructed, and the characteristic features were reproduced as closely as possible in the image. The mouth was painted red outside and black within, the teeth were shaped in pearls, and the eyes made of abalone shell with the pupils of black wax. Bunches of eagle and yellow-hammer feathers were stuck on the shoulders, and strings of beads and other ornaments disposed upon it. Around the neck was hung a net containing two small vessels with food and drink for the ghost on its journey to the spirit-world. As soon as the image was completed it was thought to be occupied by the spirit, and at the end of the fiesta (which occupied a week of ceremonial dancing) it was burned, together with offerings of blankets, clothing and other articles, in order to free the indwelling soul.

Images of the Dead

Here we have an example of the substitution of an improvised 'portrait statue' as the temporary abode of the ghost for ritual purposes, viz., while the festival lasted. When the rites had been performed the dead man no longer required an earthly habitation. Therefore, the surrogate of the body was 'cremated' to liberate its ghostly tenant. In Mexico,

[1] Turner, *Samoa* (London, 1884), page 335.

when a trader died away from home a figure of the deceased was carved in wood, ornamented, and after mourning ceremonies had been performed in conjunction with it, it was burned and the ashes were interred. This was also done in respect of warriors slain in battle. The effigy of the warrior was cremated in front of a temple and some of the ashes were sprinkled on their relatives while the rest were buried. Along the North-west Pacific coast and in British Columbia between the Skeena and Nass rivers, numerous portrait figures and posts have been found "made as life-like as possible". In one of them the cremated remains were concealed in the trunk, and at Kitzegukela on the Skeen river, the image of a man who had committed suicide was completely clothed and seated on the box that contained his ashes. In his hands were the musket and bullets with which he had shot himself. Custom dies hard. In the neighbourhood there are traditions of similar statues where men had died on the trail and been cremated leaving behind this symbol of their corporeal presence.

The fashioning of effigies of the dead regarded as the counterpart of the physical body no doubt has tended to separate the spirit from its fleshly integument, and like the practice of cremation with which it has been closely associated, it has not been without its influence on the conception of the soul as an independent entity. As long as attention is concentrated on the mortal remains and their preservation, inevitably the next life is interpreted in terms of a continuation of the physical existence. But if the life that survives the dissolution is capable of transference to some other object or body, or of returning whence it came when its temporary abode has been reduced to ashes, the way is open for a less materialistic doctrine of immortality. The primitive mind, however, being not prone to abstract thought, has never been able to conceive of survival apart from a concrete entity, be it that of a man, an animal, a spirit, or a god. Hence the prevalence of the idea of reincarnation and transmigration, the cult of heroes, and of an after-life lived in a terrestrial paradise, or on the Isles of the Blest, located often in the traditional home of the tribe, after a brief sojourn in the vicinity of the grave, usually co-extensive with the period of mourning and the transitional rites. Even when the abode of the dead is placed in the sky, or the Land of the Setting Sun, the conditions are comparable to those on earth, however idealized they may be.

The Nature and Location of the Spirit-World

Nevertheless, the spirit-world is generally regarded as a mutilated existence except in Ancient Egypt where an elaborate attempt was made to reconstitute the human organism in its several parts and attributes by a series of mechanical and ritual processes enabling it to continue its former life in its fullness in the delectable Fields of Aalu watered by the heavenly Nile, or in the celestial realms of Re where the sun never sets. In more primitive states of culture the complete personality is seldom if ever thought to be reassembled after death. Consequently, as a ghost is a phantom-like being, an image or reflection of the real man, the life of the world to come is a shadowy existence even when the transition has been successfully accomplished by the due performance of the prescribed rites.

In Melanesia, for instance, the underworld is said to be a poor place, sad and dark, where everything is unreal and shadowy, and the dead are ethereal and always enveloped in a soft cloudy mist. This doubtless explains the eagerness with which rebirth is sought whenever an opportunity occurs for the spirit-child to enter an expectant mother. Meanwhile the dead pursue their old activities and interests as best they can on the other side of the gloomy portal. Whether in the body or out of the body, death produces no essential change of character, social status or spiritual condition, and such rewards and punishments as obtain beyond the grave are confined to conspicuous heroism in battle securing for the deceased a place in a Valhalla, or in the case of certain privileged persons who attain divine or semi-divine rank, a blessed hereafter in a special paradise. But for the vast majority of mankind, the idea that the soul gains by passing out of this world is very rare indeed, and the lot of the unburied dead, or of those who die a violent death, is unenviable in the extreme.

The Mexicans thought that the spirits of women who died in childbirth became malevolent goddesses and visited the earth from time to time to lay wait for children at the crossroads in order to penetrate their bodies and so cause paralysis. When they were not engaged in these nefarious visitations they lived in the palace of the sun in the western part of the sky, and accompanied the luminary in his daily passage from midday to his setting in the West. Warriors, nobles and the emperor also dwelt in the same paradise of Uitzilopochtli, amid honeyed flowers and luscious fruits, shady groves and rich hunting parks, and escorted the sun in his daily course. After four years of this blissful Elysium they were transformed into birds with golden plumage, but the rest of the people were destined to make their bed in Mictlan, "a most obscure land where light cometh not and whence none can ever return". On reaching the ninth division at the end of the fourth year of residence in this cheerless underworld in the far north they were annihilated.

Endlessness is too abstract a concept for the primitive mind to grasp and, in consequence, it is unable to conceive of an objective life for the dead for an indefinite period. Even when the fate of the soul is not an undesirable one and admits of a measure of idealization, it is of only temporary duration. The idea of an eternal and indestructible spirit or essence lies outside its range which seldom extends beyond the few generations known to the individual. Thus, the land of the dead is the land of memory, as in Maeterlinck's fantasia, the inhabitants of which gradually pass into oblivion as the recollection of their existence becomes dim among the survivors. Periodic festivals, such as those held on three days of the year in Ancient Rome when the *mundus*, or hell's mouth on the Palatine, was opened to enable the denizens of the nether regions to visit their friends, doubtless tended to prolong their survival by keeping them in touch with their relatives.[1] But these visitations were not regarded with much favour as a general rule, and in Rome, where the dead were

[1] Festus, 156.

an unindividualized group of ancestral spirits (*manes*), the head of the household deliberately drove away the "ghosts of his fathers" at the Lemuria in May by clanging brass vessels at midnight and casting beans over his shoulder to redeem himself and his family from these unwelcome spirits.[1] At the Parentalia in February they were treated with greater civility,[2] but it was fear of their presence that caused the *mundus* to be kept closed for the greater part of the year in the State cult.

The Feast of the Dead in primitive society usually marks the end of the funerary ritual—a kind of 'year's mind'. This accomplished, all mention or even thought of the departed is forbidden except when an annual commemoration, or All Souls Day, is observed. Concerning the ultimate fate of the soul or ghost there is little or no interest, and as one member of the community after another is dispatched to the unseen world with the customary rites, gradually each in his turn is forgotten by his kinsfolk and descendants, unless it is supposed that he has returned in another body to repeat the cycle of birth, initiation and death, or, as in the case of some outstanding personality, he is raised to divine rank and venerated as a hero, ancestor or god. Occasionally, as in some modern Greek folk-tales from the Dodecanese, the hero goes to an underworld which is not the land of the dead but "the place where there are living people" ; a land we see as not ours at all, but yet belonging to a cycle of ideas entirely different from the conception of the nether world.[3]

The Influence of Culture Contact on the Cult of the Dead

Generally speaking, however, death is not an initiation into a fuller life in a progressive sequence. Rather is it a mutilated existence, a shadowy reflection of this life, with no idea of rewards and punishments based on ethical conduct. Sometimes, as in the Hebrew Sheol, all are equal, but usually

[1] Ovid, *Fasti*, v, 419-444.

[2] *Fasti*, ii, 533-570.

[3] R. M. Dawkins, *Folk-lore*, liii, 1942, pages 144ff.

there are social divisions corresponding to those on earth resulting very often from an intermingling of cultures. Thus, in the Pacific where the burial customs and beliefs in a future life have undergone considerable modification as a result of cultural migrations, two interpretations of the underworld occur, and these have been overlaid by a variety of more specialized notions. In Southern Melanesia, for instance, from Torres Straits to the New Hebrides, the land of the dead is a gloomy subterranean region, like Hades in Homer or Sheol in the Old Testament, inhabited by insubstantial shades and entered through caves or holes in the ground made by volcanic action. It is possible that this belief is associated with the earlier strata of the population of the region, and this may explain the recurrence of the belief in Polynesia among commoners, who represent the earlier population. In Indonesia and Papua, on the other hand, the subterranean abode is a more cheerful and inspiring hereafter, a kind of 'looking-glass' world where everything happens the other way round. Day becomes night, right left, black white. And in Torres Straits, with its Papuan connexions, it is a bright, happy place with splendid gardens, a belief that extends along the south coast of British New Guinea, where, in the Massim district, a mixture of Southern Melanesians and Papuan types occurs as a result of the diffusion of Melanesian culture.

In Polynesia the gloomy Melanesian underworld is inhabited by commoners who are supposed sometimes to be deaf, dumb and blind and living in utter darkness, as against the rulers who go to a special home of their own, or to an abode of the gods in the skies. But the different ideas that prevail in this area concerning the next life, and the variety of burial customs, seem to represent a fusion of the two types of belief resulting from culture contact which has been conditioned and modified by local circumstances. Nevertheless, broadly speaking alternative abodes of the dead and two sets of funeral rites among the same people may be taken as an indication of race-fusion, the spirit-world of the conquered people becoming an inferior place for less favoured souls.

At the same time it has to be remembered that such diametrically opposed practices as cremation and mummification represent fundamentally different attitudes of mind towards the dead and cannot be explained solely in terms of migration. Preservation of the body aims at keeping intact the physical integument in order that the deceased may survive in the form in which he was known in the flesh, either in the grave or in some reasonably accessible abode. Cremation, on the contrary, whatever its ostensible purpose may be, in fact represents the total destruction of all but a shadowy spiritual essence, destined usually to survive in a distant land, often located in the sky. Closely associated with this notion is the practice of destroying grave-goods to set free their spirit-parts, or soul-substance. Since ideas of the next life appear to have arisen and taken shape very largely within the framework of mortuary ritual, the accidental burning of the corpse during the ritual process of desiccation over a slow fire, and the ceremonial removal of the flesh from the decomposing body exposed for a stated period on a scaffold (a practice adopted for instance among the Choctaw east of the Mississippi), and similar customs associated with secondary burial, may have been important contributory causes in the transition from the preservation of the body to the liberation of the soul through the immolation of the flesh.

The Cult of the Dead and the Doctrine of Immortality

Death is the supreme mystery which calls forth the twofold response of attraction and repulsion. Out of this emotional tension comes the horror and dread of the corpse as a "daemonic-sacred object ritually unclean" and taboo, and, therefore, to be avoided and disposed of as summarily as possible so that a dangerous source of contagion may be removed. Conversely, it is also alluring, 'fascinating' and compelling, arousing latent emotions of love, mercy, pity and comfort, drawing the mourners into a sacramental relationship with the deceased, and making them loath to dispose of the mortal remains of a kinsman and relative. Thus arises the dual desire to shun and eliminate a dreaded object and to enter into closer relations with the mysterious 'other world' as represented by one who has crossed the veil. Out of this 'numinous' situation a complex ritual has developed in the cult of the dead which has found expression in a doctrine of immortality.

As animistic notions of a surviving soul or spirit have gradually become defined as an interpretation of the cultus, the two tendencies and reactions have been rationalized in terms of an after-life lived either in close association with the living in a preserved and restored body, generally kept at least for a time within easy reach in a grave below or above ground ; or, conversely, sent away to some ancestral home of the tribe in a distant land across the sea, or on the Western horizon. For the more privileged the Isles of the Blest are the delectable earthly paradise, and as the body ceases to be regarded as essential to the survival of the soul, its destruction may become the means of wafting the liberated spirit to the celestial realms far removed from the struggle, turmoil and limitations of terrestrial existence. But whatever may be the destiny and destination of the departed, and the procedure adopted at the time of the dissolution, the disintegrating effect of death on the solidarity of the community is stayed by the establishment of a new fellowship between the survivors and their deceased kinsmen through the cult of the dead.

BIBLIOGRAPHY

Bendann, E. *Death Customs*. London, 1930.

Bushnell, D. I. "Native Cemeteries and Forms of Burial East of the Mississippi." *71st Bulletin, Bureau of American Ethnology*. Washington, 1920.

Crawley, A. E. *The Mystic Rose*. London, 1927. New Edition by T. Besterman.

Frazer, J. G. *Belief in Immortality and the Worship of the Dead*. Vol. I–III. 1913-29. *The Fear of the Dead in Primitive Religion*. Vols. I–III. London, 1933-36.

Gennep, A. van. *Les rites de passage*. Paris, 1909.

Hartland, E. S. "Death and the Disposal of the Dead" in Hastings, *Encyclopaedia of Religion and Ethics*. Vol. IV. 1911, pp. 411-444.

James, E. O. "The Concept of the Soul in North America," *Folk-Lore.* 1927. Vol. XXXVIII, No. 4, pp. 338-358. "Cremation and the Preservation of the Dead in North America." *American Anthropologist.* 1928. N.S. Vol. XXX, No. 2, pp. 214-242.

Kroeber, A. L. "Disposal of the Dead," *American Anthropologist.* N.S. 1927. Vol. XXIX, pp. 308-315.

Malinowski, B. "Boloma, the Spirits of the Dead in the Trobriand Islands." *Journal of the Royal Anthropological Institute.* Vol. XLVI. 1916. pp. 353-430.

Moss, R. L. B. *The Life after Death in Oceania.* Oxford, 1925.

Perry, W. J. "Myths of Origin and Homes of the Dead in Indonesia." *Folk-Lore.* 1915. Vol. XXVI, pp. 138-152.

Reisner, A. L. *The Egyptian Conception of Immortality.* Boston, 1912.

Rivers, W. H. R. *The History of Melanesian Society.* Cambridge, 1914. *Psychology and Ethnology.* London, 1926. pp. 36-50.

Tylor, E. B. *Primitive Culture.* 4th Edition. London, 1903.

Yarrow, H. C. "A Further Contribution to the Study of Mortuary Customs." *1st Report, Bureau of American Ethnology.* Washington, 1881.

CHAPTER VII

MYTH AND RITUAL

AT all times and everywhere man's intense desire and determination to destroy death and 'put on immortality' has found expression not only in his ritual behaviour but also in his mythology. Thus, one has only to consult such a book as the late Sir James Frazer's *Folk-lore in the Old Testament* to see how world-wide are the stories telling how the human race originally was created immortal but by some accident, ruse or device it lost this priceless boom and became a victim of death and all the other ills to which stricken humanity has been heir throughout the ages. In our own sacred literature inherited from the Jews and given a new interpretation in Christianity, this theme is predominant and affords an illuminating example of the nature and function of myth and ritual in giving stability to faith and practice.

The Nature and Function of Myth and Ritual

When the Jewish priests retold the Babylonian story of creation in terms of the monotheistic beliefs inculcated by the Prophets after the return of the exiles to Palestine in the sixth century B.C., they did so primarily to provide a supernatural sanction for the observance of the seventh day of the week as the Sabbath. By referring back the new ritual institution to the alleged cessation of divine creative activity at the end of the first momentous week at the beginning of time, they transformed an ecclesiastical regulation into a divine decree binding on the conscience of all Jews. "For in six days the Lord made heaven and earth and rested the seventh day; wherefore the Lord blessed the Sabbath day and hallowed it." So the Genesis version of the creation myth lived on in the ritual of the nation. The Christian Church through the influence of St. Paul carried the process a stage further by reinterpreting the earlier account of the Eden disaster in relation to its own doctrine of redemption. Death being swallowed up in the victory of the Cross, paradise lost, it declared, had become paradise regained. This theme in its turn was given ritual expression in the Eucharistic sacrifice as the perpetual memorial of the supreme recreative event in the history of the world, and it became the guiding principle in the ethical conduct of the faithful. In this way the sacred story, having become incorporated in the religious and social organization of the community, lives on from age to age in its faith and practice, continually undergoing changes in meaning and significance but never ceasing to determine its worship, theology, social sanctions and morality by affording a spiritual authority and precedent for the things believed, ordered and done.

Since in primitive society the spoken word is thought to exercise supernatural power in its utterance and repetition, it gives efficacy to the actions performed and the episodes recounted as an 'uttered rite'. Emotional situations of continual recurrence require perpetual satisfaction, and around certain fundamental dogmas, such as the creation of the world, the loss of immortality and the salvation and destiny of man, a sacred narrative has developed in which the providential ordering and sustaining of all things is affirmed, and power is liberated to enable man to overcome his disabilities and shortcomings through the magic of the sacred word. The stories told and repeated with regular precision usually relate to certain events of outstanding importance which have a permanent significance in the moral, social and religious organization of society. They are not concerned with purely theoretical questions or metaphysical speculations about the ultimate beginnings of things, and they draw only to a very limited extent, if at all, upon matters of purely scientific and historical interest. Primitive people, of course, are perfectly capable of accurate observation and are constantly experimenting, improvising and improving upon their techniques, but they do not theorize or tell stories about these every-day matter-of-fact occurrences. Again, it has yet to be proved that myths represent the day-dreams of the human race giving conscious expression through an elaboration of psychoanalytic symbolism to subconscious desires, conflicts, fears and phobias. In short, primitive man is neither a philospher, a scientist nor a neurote. He is just a plain unsophisticated practical person living in a precarious environment and continually confronted with perplexing situations which he endeavours to meet as well as he is able by natural and supernatural means. His interest in the past is confined to the bearing of former events on present affairs, and when it becomes articulate in myth it is in the belief that the spoken word is an oracle the repetition of which sets free the creative and re-creative power with which it is replete.

Myths of Origin

Thus, the many stories about the way in which the present order of events came into being which recur all over the world, are certainly not the result of an innate inquisitiveness regarding the way in which the natural order has arisen, as has been supposed ;[1] neither are they imaginative episodes such as Plato had recourse to when at the end of an arduous quest for truth he felt that pure intellect had shot its bolt and yet something remained unsaid. In primitive thought myth is not called into play at the point where abstract ratiocination can go no further, any more than it is a poetic creation of fancy and of romantic story-telling like the heroic legends of Homer, Hesiod and the Epic cycle, or the body of tradition that has grown up around our British hero, Arthur, or the career of Rama in Indian lore. These are themes which lies outside the range of savage mentality, and are, in fact, the product of a long process of development and transformation. Thus, the Homeric poems are Achæan in origin and the Arthurian Cycle has come down from a pre-Roman civilization, while the great Sanskrit epic has been a national possession for at least two thousand years. As a literary production the *Mahabharata* was derived from the type of ancient legendary tale called *purana*, and the *Ramayana* from the class of artificial epic known as *kavya*, in which the poetic form is regarded as more important than the story.

The genuinely primitive myth being neither speculation nor poem, explanation nor philosophy, its ritual efficacy is the centre of interest. What happened in 'the brave days of old', and at the creation of the world, is of practical importance because it has had a permanent effect on subsequent behaviour and the structure of society. Thus, in Australia a number of initiated males are set apart for the express purpose of acting as the custodians of the tribal lore, its ritual and sacred sites. It is their business to safeguard its transmission, interpretation and correct enactment in the manner prescribed by the heroes and ancestors when they lived on the earth in the Dream Time of long ago and gave the country occupied by each group its local configuration, and ordered its laws, customs and beliefs.

[1] chf. A. Lang, *Myth, Ritual and Religion* (London, 1899), Vol. I, page 162.

This mythical past is as far back as the native traditions go, and it serves the practical purposes for which it was designed. In describing the paths along which the ancestors are supposed to have travelled, and indicating the places at which they halted to perform ceremonies, the sacredness of the existing totemic centres is affirmed and established for all time. Moreover, not only does this mythological topography 'confirm the faith' respecting the things done at the cult-centres, but it links the group with its tribal territory and provides intertribal common routes leading to the water-holes and the various sacred rites which have to be visited from time to time. The approach to them must be made along the same paths as those taken by the ancestors in the Alcheringa, or Dream Time, and as long as this course is followed the 'pilgrims,' provided they keep strictly to the peaceful purpose of their journey, are afforded protection and hospitality like those in medieval Europe en route for Santiago de Compostella (the most sacred spot in Spain which incidentally took its origin in all probability from a prehistoric megalithic monument and was approached along very ancient sacred ways).

Therefore, the myth of the wandering ancestors promotes friendly intercourse and security between local clans and tribes, and facilitates intertribal relationships. It also makes the various local groups mutually dependent for their cult-life. Each tribe is the custodian of a particular tradition and is responsible for the enactment of the myth and ritual associated with the sites in its area, thereby making its own contribution to the cultus and mythology as a composite whole. In this way the sacred lore and its rites become a consolidating force in society, grounded in the ancient past and its heroes. What they did during their wanderings and sojourn on earth in the Dream Time must be done now by their descendants because upon the due performance of this ancestral cultus at the proper places depends the well-being of the tribe. So the myth lives on in its ritual, and the creative period of long ago is an ever-present reality, re-enacted in the traditional manner on the great ceremonial occasions.

By grounding the established order in a mythological supernatural reality, stability is given to the social structure and religious organization, making them proof against the disintegrating forces of change and decay. So long as it is believed that the regulations respecting marriage, for example, were laid down once and for all by the ancestors in the beginning, no departure from the rules is possible, any more than in the performance of the traditional rites which have been similarly prescribed and rationalized in the current mythology. If the complicated rules governing the kinship system came into being in this way, that is sufficient reason in the native mind for their observance and continuance, because the laws ordained at the threshold of human history must be observed having then been fixed for all time. This is the essence of tribal morality of which mythology is the guardian.

Cosmological Myths

Closely connected with the mythology of a formative period in which the laws, institutions, customs and beliefs were bestowed upon mankind by ancestral beings, is the creation story describing the transformation of the earth into its present form by a beneficent Originator or Transformer, who assumes the rôle either of a Culture hero or of a Supreme Being. Since, as we have seen, the High God tends to be remote and little concerned with the government and sustenance of the world, he figures less prominently in this type of traditional lore than the more intimate subordinates to whom he delegates his creative functions.

Not infrequently in these cosmological myths, as in the Hebrew story of the Garden of Eden, the existence of the earth, or of the material universe, is taken for granted. Moreover, as the problem of ultimate origins and the idea of creation *ex nihilo* lies outside the range of the primitive mind, it is usually assumed that all things have come into being out of existing materials, such as the primeval ocean from which the earth was 'fished up', or fashioned in some way or another. According to the Crow Indians of Montana in

North America, "long ago there was no earth, only water. The only creatures in the world were the ducks and Old Man" (i.e., the Sun as the Supreme Being who has become merged with the Transformer known as the Coyote). "He came down to meet the ducks and said to them, 'My brothers, there is earth below us. It is not good for us to be alone' ". They were then told to dive into the waters and out of the mud collected in the webbed feet of one of them he created the earth. "Now that we have created the earth," he said, "there are others who wish to be animate". Immediately a wolf appeared and the world was peopled with living creatures.

In Central California, where the Coyote figures very prominently in the mythology as a co-creator, transformer, evil genius and puck-like trickster, both he and the Supreme Being are generally represented as appearing on the primeval waters in a mysterious manner, as if from nowhere. This is the nearest approach to the idea of creation *ex nihilo*, except perhaps in the Uitoto myth of Colombia, South America, in which it is asserted that in the beginning only 'appearance' existed as a phantasm out of which Nainema, 'He who is appearance only,' brought all things into being through a dream. In California among the Achomawi both the Creator and Coyote emerged in the condensation of a primeval fog, while in the neighbouring Maidu, who lived formerly in the Sacramento Valley and the Sierra Nevada, they descended upon the waters in a canoe.

On the West Coast of Southern Australia darkness and silence are said to have reigned over the mountains and valleys concealing static forms of life until the Great Spirit awoke the Sun-goddess and whispered to her to animate the universe. Thereupon she took a great breath that caused the atmosphere to vibrate, opened her eyes and her whole body became flooded with light. Darkness disappeared and when she made her home on the plain her vitalizing influence began to be felt upon the cold life of earth. As she walked in a Westerly direction the shrubs and trees sprang up in her footprints. She repeated her journeys all over the earth until it was covered with vegetation. Next she set out to take warmth and brightness to the cold regions in the caverns out of which emerged snakes and lizards. Butterflies, beetles and animals of all shapes, sizes and colours began to appear, and the seasonal changes, together with the succession of light and darkness, were ordained. Her work completed, the goddess returned to the sky and stood smiling upon them from her celestial abode, moving from East to West, and finally disappeared as darkness fell at night. She appointed the morning star to rule as her son, and the moon as the lady of the night to help him to shine in the darkness as his wife. They brought forth children who took their places in the sky as stars.

These cosmological myths of Southern and Eastern Australia in which sky heroes play the principal rôles, perform the same sociological functions as those of the Alchera ancestors in the Central and North-western regions. In these stories the work of creation was completed by a single figure, the First Father, to whom the Sun-goddess gave all power to finish the task she had begun. Sometimes he is equated with the moon which waxes and wanes like the first mortal who lives, dies and is restored. He is also symbolized under the form of semi-mythical animals, as in the case of the hares, rabbits, snakes and lizards which renew their youth by changing their skins, or some similar device. In his creative capacity, however, he has become equated with the Supreme Being and assumed many of his attributes so that it is often difficult to distinguish the one from the other. In a Yuki myth in California, for instance, the vault of the sky is stretched out by the combined efforts of the High God and the Culture-hero and supported on four great pillars at the cardinal points. A path is left for the sun and openings for the rain and mist to descend on the earth. Man is moulded out of clay and then the sun and moon, wind and rain are called into being. A flood destroys all men and animals, and the work is finished by the re-creation of life, and to the complete satisfaction of the Creator and his faithful dog. In another version of the story, a being called Thunder is said to have lived alone in the upper sky-world until he found a baby wrapped in leaves who became the progenitor of the human race, very much as among the Wichita of Texas the High God only bestowed the potentialities of all things in the beginning leaving it to the First Man to cause the sun and moon to appear, acting under a divine impulse.

The same theme recurs in a Pawnee tale in the state of Nebraska. When the all-powerful sky-chief, Tirawa, decided to create the earth he disclosed his plans to the gods and gave them their several stations. The sun was told to stand in the east to give light and warmth to the earth ; the moon was to stand in the west to give light during the hours of darkness ; and the evening star was to be there also as the Mother of all things, for through her all things would be created. This was accomplished by the four gods singing and so producing a cloud into which Tirawa dropped a pebble. The space was filled with water out of which the four gods made the world and prepared it for habitation. Animals and plants having been created, the first men and women came down from the sky, the son of the Sun and the daughter of the Evening-star, the sky-goddess. From them the human race is descended and has derived its rites and customs. Thus, while the High God is the ultimate source of creative activity, he employs intermediaries to exercise his powers and dispense his gifts in the world he and his associates have called into being. "All the powers that are in the heavens and all those that are upon the earth are derived," we are told, "from the mighty power of Tirawa. He is the father of all things visible and invisible. He is the father of all the powers represented by the Hako . . and perpetuates the life of the tribe through the gift of children".[1]

Therefore, this ceremony, called the Hako, is held in the spring when the birds are mating, in the summer when they are rearing their young, in the autumn when they are flocking, and in the winter when they are asleep, to obtain from the High God "the gift of life, of strength, of plenty and of peace". Embodied in some twenty rituals consisting of dances, songs and mimetic actions, is the dramatization of

[1] A. Fletcher, *22nd Report of the Bureau of American Ethnology* (Washington, 1904), Part II, page 107.

the creation story reproducing on earth the world of the gods as it existed when the present order was established. This is made clear in a ceremony which the Skidi group of the Pawnee perform in their sacred enclosure portraying the community of the gods in the sky. In the centre is a fireplace surrounded by four posts placed respectively to the north-east, south-east, south-west and north-west. At the west end is a raised altar of earth inside the enclosure, and at the east end outside the enclosure is a mound. A priest is stationed at each of the posts and at the fireplace impersonating the gods at the cardinal points in the creation story.[1] Fire being the earthly counterpart of the sun, the symbol of life and of the orderly sequence of events,[2] the sacred fireplace occupies the central position in the rite and its setting, while the posts represent the supports of the domed roof of the sky, symbolised in the mount outside the enclosure.

This symbolism, in fact, may still be observed in many churches in our own land where the altar, taking the place of the fireplace in the Pawnee ceremonial ground, often is enclosed by four riddel posts and surmounted with a dome-like canopy, or *ciborium*, painted with stars on a blue surface on the underside in imitation of the sky. In ascending the steps of the sanctuary the sacred ministers go as it were into the heavenly sphere to "join with angels and archangels and the whole company of heaven" in offering the Holy Sacrifice in union with the eternal High Priest, who, having passed through the veil, is exalted at the right hand of the Majesty on high. It is this theme, or something very like it, that underlies the Pawnee ceremonial.

The rite is believed to have been given to the ancestors of the tribe at the threshold of its history, as in the case of the Australian mysteries, and in it is re-enacted the drama of creation exactly as it was handed down from the mysterious

[1] J. R. Murie, *Anthropological Papers of the Natural History of America*, Vol. XI, 1916, pages 351ff.

[2] e.g., In the Vedic ritual in India fire is equated both with the sun and with the ritual and moral order of the universe established creatively through sacrifice.

powers above. None of the actions or songs can be changed, for the gestures and words must be repeated precisely in the form in which they were delivered by the gods in the beginning as the means whereby the potency of Tirawa was bestowed upon mankind through his intermediaries, as the centre and source of fertility and of the tribal unity. Thus, the primeval drama lives on in the prescribed ritual and makes it an efficacious sign of creative activity and the consolidating force in the social structure.

Creation to the primitive mind does not convey the idea of a 'First Cause' in the sense understood, for instance, by the Deists in the seventeenth and eighteenth centuries of our era ; still less that of a beginning *in* time or *of* time. It involves rather the notion of renovating and revivifying the existing order of things to render the earth habitable and serviceable for human needs and organized for the well-being of society. The sacred order being the ground and support of the world and not merely its beginning, without it it could not exist at any moment. For this reason it sees the operation of divine forces in every natural event, and by referring institutional observances back to their original source in the transcendental world recreative energy is liberated. The repetition of the myth of creation and its re-enactment in a sacred drama revitalizes and renews the face of the earth. To tell how a beneficent Providence as the giver of the laws of life and of all that is good exercised his functions in the beginning, is to impart a new vigour to the creative processes when it is believed that a spoken narrative possesses decisive efficacious power in its repetition, comparable to that of the sacred action. The essence of myth, in fact, lies in its being repeatedly told anew to give intention to the things done, and release in perpetuity the initial power recalled by the narrative of past events, celebrated as a living reality in the present.

Seasonal Mythology

Thus, the daily course of nature and the regular succession of the seasons are given mythological form and expression in agricultural communities in relation to the vegetation cultus. The sequence upon which the growth of the crops depends must be maintained and its vitality retained by the celebration of the cult-drama in which the events which are supposed to have happened in primeval times are recalled in a myth and re-enacted in a ritual to renew the processes of fertility and stabilize the social and religious organization on which the community depends for its well-being and sustenance. The same methods are employed, and often the same words are repeated, as those supposed to have been used by the original Creator or Transformer in the formative period of the world's history to release their potency by recapitulation.

In the great collection of myths and liturgies that recur in the texts belonging to the third and second millenia B.C. in Asia Minor, Mesopotamia, Egypt, and Palestine, the victory of the beneficent forces at the threshold of creation is set forth and enacted in terms of a primeval struggle between gods. In the Tammuz liturgies, for example, the death of the king-god, Tammuz, at the hands of a supernatural adversary is described, followed by his imprisonment in the underworld, the lamentation of his sister-wife, Ishtar, who went to the nether regions in search of her lover, and his triumphant return to earth, symbolizing the yearly decay and revival of vegetation. In the urban civilization of Babylonia, as we have seen, the myth is re-enacted at the Annual Festival called *Akitu* with Marduk having replaced Tammuz and the ancient Sumerian Creation Epic, which goes back to about 3000 B.C., occupying a central position as the basic myth of the New Year ritual.

In this later version, known as the *Enuma elish*, as set forth in the cuneiform texts of the eighth century B.C., it has undergone a good deal of revision at the hands of the Babylonian priests to bring it into line with the story and significance of Marduk as a solar city-god, but its main theme and purpose remains essentially unchanged as an integral part of a seasonal drama, the ceremonial of which belongs at least to the time of Sargon (*c.* 2500 B.C.). In the Babylonian festival it was recited to give life to the god (Marduk), to re-install and re-invigorate the king as his human representative, and to fix the 'destinies' (i.e., maintain the cosmic order) for the coming year, just as in the original rite Tammuz, or Dumu-zi, "the true son of the waters" (i.e., the life-giver), put an end to blight, dearth and death by rising from a watery grave by the aid of Ishtar, reborn from the underworld.

In the Babylonian epic of the adventures of the hero Gilgamesh, king of Erech, with whom Ishtar is said to have fallen in love, the story of the deluge has been incorporated as an incident in his search for immortality. Behind the narrative and its Sumerian prototypes, there would appear to have been a historical situation since archæological excavation has now brought to light evidence of an extensive flood in Mesopotamia in the neighbourhood of Ur and Kish about 3000 B.C. of a magnitude unparalleled in local experience.[1] But in its mythological form the event is interpreted as a sort of *rite de passage* in which Ut-Naphistim, the ancestor of Gilgamesh, passed through the waters of death in order to attain immortality. Therefore, apparently it acquired a ritual significance as part of the death and resurrection drama, the hero rising to newness of life like Tammuz emerging from the waters. Moreover, in the Sumerian version we are told that "after the Flood kingship again descended from heaven", while in the subsequent Hebrew record in the book of Genesis, the deluge is represented as a re-creative act in which Yahweh initiated a new post-diluvian epoch in the history of the world with Noah as the ancestor of the new humanity (Gen. ix, 1, 8ff.).

In the ritual texts recently discovered at Ras Ṣhamra on the north Syrian coast, written in an alphabetic script closely allied to Hebrew and ascribed to the fourteenth century B.C., or perhaps earlier (*c.* 1500), the Tammuz cult-drama recurs, probably in the form of a liturgy. The dying and rising god reappears in the guise of a fertility deity, Aleyan son of Baal, who is killed in the spring by his enemy Mot, the god of the harvest and son of El, the Lord of the underworld. This produces the drought of summer, and in order to ensure the return of the fertilizing showers of autumn, Aleyan-Baal

[1] C. L. Woolley, *Ur of the Chaldees* (London, 1929), pages 22ff.

has to be restored to life after the harvest, and Mot in his turn is killed and his flesh is scattered over the fields as a kind of manure, like that of the dismembered body of Osiris in the Egyptian myth. The "fixing of the destinies" in the Tammuz-Marduk story has its counterpart in the Ras Shamra texts in the acquisition of certain magical objects called teraphim to secure the proper functioning of the processes of nature, and there are several indications of a sacred marriage having been celebrated in honour of the victory of the god.[1]

The persistence and widespread distribution of this myth and ritual are to be explained by the fact that they represent a recurrent situation of profound emotional significance in the life of agricultural communities dependent upon the weather and the seasons for their subsistence. Therefore, whether the dying and reviving god was called Tammuz, Adonis, Aleyan-Baal, Osiris or Dionysos, the same drama was enacted to regenerate nature at its most vital centre, symbolized by the death and revival of the divine hero and his earthly embodiment, the king. But in Egypt, as we have seen, Osiris was the Lord of the dead as well as the personification of growth and fertility, and in the other versions of the theme the underworld figures prominently. This doubtless explains why the mystery cultus, when it spread to Greece in the sixth century B.C., acquired a more individual character as the means whereby the initiates were assured of a blessed resurrection after death.

Folk Drama

These cults survived in Western Europe until the opening centuries of the Christian era, and before they were finally submerged in the new faith and practice they had exercised considerable influence on Christian doctrine and ritual. The Mass became the sacred drama *par excellence* as the perpetual commemoration of the death and resurrection of Christ, the renewal day by day of His redemptive sacrifice, and the

[1] cf. Hooke, *The Origins of Early Semitic Ritual* (Oxford, 1935), pages 28ff.

'medicine of immortality' dispensed in Holy Communion. But, as has been pointed out in another connexion, the liturgy in due course gave rise to dramatic performances, ostensibly sacred in character and origin, but which tended to become secularised in the course of time. At first they were held in church, then in the churchyard, and eventually in the market-place, where more and more they lost their original content, until at length they merged with the rustic revels which survived in the peasant culture, little changed from the beginnings of agricultural civilization.

Thus, for example, as recently as 1906 Professor Dawkins discovered in Thrace a folk play in which the ancient Dionysiac myth and ritual were still performed annually at the carnival in the villages round Veza, between Adrianople and Estanbul. Two men in goatskins and masks visited all the houses, knocking on the doors with a fertility symbol in the form of a phallus, and carrying a cross-bow. Two boys dressed as brides danced outside the house, while a gipsy man and his wife performed an obscene pantomime and pretended to forge a ploughshare. A man, disguised as an old unmarried woman in rags, called 'Babo,' carrying in a cradle (*liknon*) a mock baby supposed to be seven months old and illegitimate, appeared on the scene at this point. The play opened with the child growing at great pace, developing an enormous appetite and demanding a wife. A mock marriage ensued with one of the 'brides,' and the bridegroom was then shot with the bow by the second of the two goatskin men. Loud lamentation followed and the 'corpse' was lifted up as if to be carried to the grave, but instead the dead man suddenly came to life and jumped up on his feet.

The death and resurrection drama ended, a ploughshare was again supposed to be fashioned by the gipsy man, and two small boys were yoked to a real plough which they dragged twice round the village square widdershins (i.e., against the sun). At its tail walked one of the goatskin men, at the front the other man similarly attired, while a third man followed scattering seed from a *liknon* (basket). On the third round the gipsy and his wife replaced the boys, and the people shouted, "May wheat be ten piastres the bushel. Amen O God, that the poor folk may eat! Yea, O God that the poor folk be filled!"[1]

That this Thracian play held in the spring just before Lent was the dramatization of the Dionysiac celebrated in ancient Greece at Athens at the end of February, is suggested by the wonder-child born of an unmarried mother and laid in a winnowing fan, or *liknon*, as Dionysos was called *Liknites*, 'he of the cradle'. Its illegitimacy may be a relic of the miraculous birth of the divine hero, and his death, resuscitation and espousal to a bride, simulates the union of heaven and earth for the renewal of life in the spring 'that the poor may eat.' The phallic procession, the obscene pantomime, the circumstances surrounding the child, the combat, the re-animation ceremony and the marriage, have their counterparts not only in Dionysian myth and ritual but in folk drama everywhere.

Thus, in the Mumming plays the central act is the fight between two or more opponents, usually called the King, or St. George, and Turkey Knight, one or all of whom are killed or wounded amid loud lamentation and then restored to life by a Doctor. The play ends with universal rejoicing. As a serio-comic survival of the seasonal drama it has preserved the main theme, viz., the death and resurrection of the royal hero-god, and added burlesque characters, such as the doctor's man, Jack Finney, the Man-woman, Beelzebub (Belzey Bob), Bob Slasher, Little Johnnie Jack, Little David Dout, Father Christmas and so on, devoid of any obvious function. The leaders of the once mighty forces of good and evil have become farcical figures, sometimes carrying a club or a dripping pan, while the tremendously serious sacred marriage has degenerated into a functionless 'man-woman', or 'boy-girl' character. The fallen hero has descended to the level of a farcical St. George, and the masked impersonators of the gods are merely clowns with bladders, blackened faces and calves' tails. The hobby-horse may belong to the same category, unless it represents the last relic of animal sacrifice. But it is the combat and its sequel

[1] R. M. Dawkins, *Journal of Hellenic Studies*, XXVI, 1906, pages 192-201.

that give the clue to the original meaning and purpose of Folk drama and the Sword dance.

When myth and ritual no longer exercise their proper function in society in the formation and maintenance of the social order, they rapidly degenerate into idle tales told for amusement and conventional ceremonial which at best is merely quaint and picturesque, or an excuse for healthy exercise, as in the case of the folk dance. Around historical figures, *legends* (as distinct from myths) tend to cling, providing heroes with a halo of romance, just as they enhance the prestige of saints and sanctuaries. Being attached to actual persons and places they preserve a considerable element of fact, whereas when a myth ceases to be a reality lived, embodied in a rite and in the social structure, it has no other useful purpose to fulfil. Consequently, it either lives on as an adjunct of peasant culture in the form of folklore, or it comes to an end ingloriously as burlesque or superstition.

Folklore

The term 'Folklore' was coined in 1846 by T. H. Thoms to take the place of the rather awkward expression 'Popular Antiquities', which hitherto had been used to describe the oral traditions and culture of the unlettered classes in civilized communities, comprising beliefs, customs, institutions, pastimes, sayings, songs, ballads, stories and arts and crafts, both as regards their origin and their present social functions. In this rich field of inquiry, John Aubrey had led the way as early as 1686 when, in his *Remaines of Gentilisme and Judaisme* he gave an account of such practices current in his day as 'sin-eating' and making offerings in kind at funerals. In 1725 Henry Bourne recorded in a little book entitled *Antiquitates Vulgares* the 'opinions and ceremonies' observed in the neighbourhood of Newcastle-on-Tyne. From this unpretentious beginning, half a century later sprang the volumes which subsequently were known as John Brand's *Observations on Popular Antiquities in Great Britain.* These were followed, in 1826, by Hone's *Everyday Book*, and in Germany by the remarkable collections of folk-tales, or *märchen*, in Jakob Grimm's *Deutsche Mythologie* (1812-15).

It was left, however, to the well-known Sanskrit scholar Max Müller and to A. Kuhn to make the study of mythology a crucial issue by tracing its origin to a 'disease of language'. From a comparative study of the Indian Rig Veda, the Iranian Avesta, the Scandinavian Edda and the Homeric literature, they endorsed the view of the brothers Grimm that both mythology and language are rooted deep in the heart of the common people, and are not the creation of the higher ranks in society. The explanation of myths is to be sought, they supposed, in nature and the heavenly bodies, notably the sun, and this it was claimed could be established by a philological analysis of mythical names. Wilhelm Mannhardt, on the other hand, having set himself systematically to collect, compare and explain the living customs and beliefs of the peasantry, concentrated attention upon the vegetation cultus of the farmer and the woodman. It now appeared that the oldest material was to be found not in the solar myths but in analogies of the classical stories with the German wood-maidens and the animistic spirits of the corn and of the wild. In England the parallel movement, initiated by the animistic theory of Tylor which influenced Mannhardt's interpretation of rural customs and beliefs, reached its climax in Frazer's monumental work, *The Golden Bough*, the first edition of which appeared in 1890.

In seeking to elucidate the unexplained rule of the Arician priesthood of Diana at her sylvan shrine on the banks of lake Nemi in the Alban hills, Frazer found in the sacrifice of the divine king the secret of the mysterious figure of the guardian of the 'golden bough', or mistletoe, reigning in lonely seclusion 'beneath Aricia's trees' as 'the priest who slew the slayer, and shall himself be slain'. The attempt to settle this question, however, raised many more problems, and step by step the indefatigable author was lured on, as he tells us, into far-spreading fields of primitive thought which had been little explored by his predecessors.

The evidence brought to light by Frazer, Tylor, Mannhardt and Andrew Lang, and their collaborators, destroyed once and for all the philological speculations of Max Müller and his followers, but no serious attempt was made to distinguish the lore of the folk embedded in civilizations from the myth and ritual of the savage living under genuinely primitive conditions. It remained for the late Sir Lawrence Gomme to draw this distinction, and to insist that the historical development of each culture must be taken into account before any analysis, classification or comparison is made between their customs, rites and beliefs.[1] It is unscientific, he maintained, to compare observances and traditions found among the European peasantry with those of the aboriginal populations on the fringes of civilization, although the religious institutions of both may have had a common origin. In the process of development, the divergence between the two cultures has been too great to make possible a legitimate comparison between the resultant products. On the other hand, a belief found among the folk may well be compared, in his opinion, with a belief recorded in classical mythology, the Rig Veda or the Avesta, since the cultural level, he thought, was much the same.

Apart from the vexed question of the historical value of folk material, its importance as an integral element in a *living* culture can hardly be over-emphasized. As a vital part of the life of the peasantry, arising out of their religious, social and economic tradition, customs, songs, stories, arts and crafts, reveal their mind and creative genius. Under modern conditions this phase of culture is so rapidly disappearing everywhere that it is ceasing to be the direct expression of its subject-matter, and tending more and more to become either interesting 'bygones' or unedifying superstitions devoid of any serious meaning and purpose, like palmistry, crystal gazing, and beliefs about 'luck'. Unorganized and detached survivals from a former state of organic development, as in the case of the vermiform appendix and similar vestigial organs, are a cause of embarrassment to the organism unless they can be utilized in some beneficial manner and so acquire a functional value. Rites which were once 'faith' but which, from a later and higher cultural standpoint, have simply 'remained over,' become the equivalent of the Latin '*superstitio*,' which perhaps is best translated by the English term

[1] *Folk-lore as an Historical Science* (London, 1908).

'survival' rather than 'superstition'. But however the phenomenon be defined, it ceases to exercise its proper function in detachment from the life of the community in which it occurs.

The efforts made in recent years to resuscitate the Folk-play, the Folk-dance and the Folk-song can hardly hope to restore their original significance in society. The drama often has been derived from printed sources and the actors may be no longer men of the soil, while even rural festivals, like folk-tales, are apt to lose their spontaneity and become an escape from life rather than a reproduction of it. The folk-dance frequently is now a pastime of the sophisticated, as is the folk-song, but, nevertheless, the fact that they make such a ready appeal in a mechanized age, so far removed from the culture in which they arose, is an indication of their vitality and the continuity of the emotions to which they give expression in action and words. Beneath the very thin veneer of modernity the living pulse of the folk still can be felt.

Moreover, in rural communities traditional ways of life and thought still survive as an integral part of a living culture, while many trades and industries have retained their own beliefs, customs and institutions (e.g., fisherfolk, sailors, landworkers, miners, etc.), which are as illuminating as they are culturally significant. In the material sphere, folk arts and crafts throw valuable light on the life and work of a people before the Industrial Revolution, and, therefore, the establishment of Folk Museums—an enterprise in which the Scandinavian countries have taken the lead—is to be welcomed as illustrating the evolution of society in its more material aspects for several hundred years. From these visible expressions of the folk mind valuable hints often can be obtained concerning the lore, learning and religion of former ages. For all these reasons, in the elucidation of the nature and origin of human institutions and beliefs the same care should be given to the study of the European peasant cultures, and their counterparts elsewhere, as to those of the more remote primitive peoples in Australia, Africa and the Pacific.

While there is no master key which will release all the

secrets of the beginnings of religion, and much must remain hidden away in obscurity, lost for ever in the remote recesses of primeval origins, a judicial use of the data made available in recent years by archæological excavation, anthropological inquiry and the investigation of the folk cultures of modern civilizated communities, renders it possible to arrive at certain general conclusions respecting the raw material of religion and the function it has fulfilled in the development of society and in laying the foundation of the spiritual understanding of mankind. If at this stage ritual dominates the situation, this is only because the deepest emotions of the human heart, and the most profound convictions of the mind, find expression in actions before they are given utterance in words and elaborated in systematized theologies and philosophies, ætiological mythologies, spiritualized worship and ethical rules of conduct. Our purpose in this volume has been to determine the rudimentary ideas of religion and its fundamental practices in their historical, sociological and psychological context, leaving it to the other writers in this series to tell the rest of the fascinating story of the quest of the human spirit for fellowship with the transcendental source of its being, and of all becoming starting from these lowly beginnings.

BIBLIOGRAPHY

Burne, C. S. *The Handbook of Folk-lore.* London, 1914. (2nd Edition.)

Chambers, E. K. *The Mediaeval Stage.* Oxford, 1903.

Cornford, F. M. *The Origin of Attic Comedy.* London, 1914.

Elkin, A. P. *The Australian Aborigines.* Sydney and London, 1938.

Folk-lore. Transactions of the Folk-lore Society, and its other publications.

Frazer, J. G. *Folk-lore in the Old Testament.* London, 1918. 3 vols.

Gomme, G. L. *Folk-lore as a Historical Science.* London, 1908.

Halliday, W. R. *Greek and Roman Folk-lore.* New York, 1927. *Folk-lore Studies, Ancient and Modern.* London, 1924.

Hocart, A. M. "The Life-giving Myth" in *The Labyrinth.* Ed. S. H. Hooke. London, 1935. *Kingship.* Oxford, 1927.

Hooke, S. H. *Myth and Ritual.* Oxford, 1933. *The Origins of Early Semitic Ritual.* London, 1935.
Hull, E. *Folk-lore in the British Isles.* London, 1928.
James, E. O. *Christian Myth and Ritual.* London, 1933.
Krappe, A. H. *The Science of Folk-lore.* London, 1930.
Lang, A. *Myth, Ritual and Religion.* London, 1899.
Malinowski, B. *Myth in Primitive Psychology.* London, 1936.
Marett, R. R. *Psychology and Folk-lore.* London, 1920.
Pollard, A. W. *English Miracle Plays, Moralities and Interludes.* Oxford, 1923.
Radcliffe Brown, A. *The Andaman Islanders.* Cambridge, 1927.
Radin, P. *Primitive Religion.* London, 1938.
Schmidt, W. *High Gods in North America.* Oxford, 1933.
Spencer, B. *The Arunta.* London, 1927.
Tiddy, R. J. E. *The Mummers' Play.* Oxford, 1923.

FINIS

INDEX

(f) denotes footnote.